EIRINI PRESS

C000120140

Optimism

The Lesson Of Ages

*A compendium of democratic theology,
designed to illustrate necessities
whereby all things are as they are,
And to reconcile the discontents of men
with the perfect love and power of
Ever-present god.*

By Benjamin Paul Blood

"Eureka."—*The Fool*

Eirini Press (Eirinipress.com)
510 Long Hill Rd.
Guilford, CT 06437

Eirini Press—exploring reawakenings to wholeness

Optimism was first published by Bela Marsh, Boston, 1860.

©2009: Foreword

Library of Congress Control Number: 2009926673
Optimism/Benjamin Paul Blood

ISBN 978-0-9799989-1-1
    1. Blood, Benjamin Paul
    2. Religion: Spirituality, Mysticism

CONTENTS

Foreword

ℬenjamin Paul Blood (1832-1919) is perhaps best known as a formative mystical influence on William James. The son of a wealthy landowner, Blood lived in Amsterdam, NY. While not committed to any one profession, he had an early interest in inventing and held patents for a reaping machine and a reinforced side saddle. His writing became a constant through his adult life, the bulk of which was in the form of letters and columns for a variety of newspapers in an era when the discourse was much like today's blogs. Through the newspapers, Blood was able to bring his philosophical ideas to a churchgoing public that he considered largely immoral.

Although initially receiving a lukewarm response, Blood's most influential work, especially on William James, was the *Anaesthetic Revolution and the Gist of Philosophy* (1874), a 37-page pamphlet expounding on the mystical revelations prompted by the taking of ether. The work also struck a chord with Tennyson, who wrote to Blood,

> I never had any revelations through anaesthetics, but a
> kind of "waking trance" (this for lack of a better word) I
> have frequently had quite up from boyhood, when I had

been all alone. This has often come upon me through re-
peating my own name to myself silently, till all at once,
as it were, out of the consciousness of individuality, the
individuality itself seemed to dissolve and fade away into
foundless being—and this not a confused state, but the
clearest of the clearest, the surest of the surest, utterly
beyond words—whose death was an almost laughable
impossibility—the loss of personality (if so it were)
seeming no extinction, only true life.*

Blood also published several volumes of poetry, as well as
an essay, *Pluriverse*, published posthumously.

An early work, *Optimism* was published in 1860, the
same year as (but presumably written prior to) Blood's
first ether experience. It reveals that even the pre-ether-
ized Blood was already challenging the common spiritual beliefs of his time as well as common sense notions of
consciousness. The work was well received by Emerson,
Wendell Phillips, and others.

Always an outsider to the academy, Blood relished
his role as a maverick, unafraid to shock mainstream
theology. Robert W. Marks, in his 1953 dissertation,
called *Optimism* "… a plain affirmation of the proposition that religious experience must precede religious
knowledge."

Impassioned by his mystical experiences, *Optimism*
demonstrates Blood as mystic of the timeless nondual

*From a letter printed in the *Utica Herald* December 4, 1874, and reprinted
in the *New York Times* two days later.

philosophy speaking in a distinctly American voice: It's all God—the good and the bad. Know that, all can be endured, and all burdens are lifted.

Later work shows that Blood wavered a bit under the influence of James' pluralism and exploration of various other philosophers. Yet his presentation of the grand consciousness, designed by God, encompassing all of us as one, did not waver. As he wrote in *Optimism:* "The burden of all theology has been to find the reason of pain in the present life, and to find hope in a life that shall be joyful, through the unwavering love of God." Blood argues that self, free will, time and evil are all part of the illusion God created to help us along, and he systematically attempts to reconcile individual perceptions of reality in daily life with his mystically revealed monism:

> We easily conceive ourselves invested in bodies or spheres of palpitating, ethereal lightness, which may fly, at will, around the pendant world; yet the sense in which we were independent of God's consciousness in our own would be as mysterious as now. However we exist, doubtless we shall feed only upon his bounty, and shall never inspire ourselves.

Prior to the widespread dissemination of eastern nonduality in western print, Blood echoed the truths of the Vedanta, Zen Buddhism, and Greek philosophers such as Parmenides and Plotinus in the language of post-Puritan, evangelical America. While the evidence of his study of western philosophy is evident throughout the volume, what may seem like allusions to eastern canons appear to be of his own experience, as he, like most Americans in the nineteenth century, had little knowledge of comparative religions. His conclusion about suffering is distinctly his own—

> When we undertake to pass upon the propriety of God's dealings with us, we must still bear in mind a former position: that we, as finite beings, cannot comprise any perfect system as individuals; we are but imperfect parts of one entire perfect system.

When we have sifted through Blood's nineteenth-century syntax, we find that perhaps the New Age is not so new. Everyday Americans of the 1800s experienced shifts in consciousness just as modern meditators and mystical Christians do. Blood's cultural and theological filter expressed his conviction of one interconnected whole in terms of Christianity, the monopolistic theology of mid-nineteenth century America.

In the end, Blood admits that while no one can know ultimate truth for certain, faith in God's cosmic plan is a comfort and source of inspiration that can guide us.

— *Denise L. Meyer*

Section I.

Some Question Of the Author's Ability

A fancy overtakes us at times to question our presumption in writing a book. Wherein are we better than another, that we should attempt to doctor another? We look over the matter-of-fact world and find it impossible to make a show, unless we have something to exhibit: yet here are we who can fiddle little, and fife less—who cannot turn somersets, as we could once when we were less fit to write a book—who cannot commit by the page like an actor, nor play chess with a third-rate,—in short who cannot prove our ability by any standard feat whatsoever, proposing to indoctrinate many who can do all these things into the deepest mysteries of life! It is indeed a question, Why should we write a book?—We have but one encouragement without our own conceit, which is, that few, if any, of the accepted wits of the past were ever excellent in the positive feats which we have mentioned. They seem to have possessed an acknowledged greatness in their general health, harmony, or proportion of mind, to whose consciousness pleasant truth was congenial, and came through some subtlety of attraction. This harmony or health of soul must comprise something of that delicate presence called *genius:* and here is our encouragement—that although we have few, if any, notable specialities to boast of, we may have a very excellent genius nevertheless.

And if it shall be found that even genius, to possess truth, must go about and court its vicinity somewhat, we shall exalt our horn a little, because of experience of various sorts that we have encountered more than most writers—experience of the varieties and extremities of outer and inner life. In this particular we can boast of having been poor enough to believe that appetite was ever sufficient, and that means to gratify it were the only requisites of contentment,—and rich enough to wish us compelled to hard labor to win again the appetites that once annoyed us. So our book may have in it the wit of both wealth and poverty. We have lain at death's door and knocked for admission; and we have wished to live on earth forever. So our book may contain the wisdom of health and of sickness. We have been heartsick, melancholy, and despairing for months; and we have known spirits for years together which have defied calamity, pain, and care, and in which even now we are taking our immortality at leisure. So our book may contain something of madness if not of sanity. And we have held many opinions in course, and followed many occupations: we have been actor, artist, solicitor, playwright, poet, metaphysician, farmer and machinist; we have lectured, published, and preached a little; we have showed, gambled, and shyed our cap in the prize ring. Surely our book shall have the wit of the vagabond.—To the philanthropist who would reproach so reckless and aimless a life, there is this consolation, that it hath compassed but twenty-eight years, by God's mercy; and time seems left us to amend. Yet for our own sake we would not recall nor re-live one hour of the past, if this book's success shall crown our martyred respectability—which, living, had kept us incompetent to the task before us. We have heard that the rolling stone gathers no moss; but we shall have lived to learn that the polish of locomotion compensates the want of the rich moss that grows only on quiet and stability, and shall flatter ourself that only a stone of some symmetry has any tendency to roll. We shall say that a man is wiser for a diversified experience; that he must have learned, better than any one-idea man, the features of humanity, and the spirit of the democratic life; that a man whose notions of the world are drawn from the expurgated editions of a circulating library—who never has sought the byways of life—who never was very sick nor very well, very rich nor very poor, who never was drunk, mad, moonstruck nor ecstatic, in short who knows little by experience of the varieties and extremities of life and consciousness, cannot stand before us as an exponent of human sentiments, nor tell how much a man's theology (especially his own) is suffering for want of an extended observation.—But let all this be as it may: we ask no charity to our errors, and deprecate no censure of our follies. The book shall be our defence;—and if we shall live to think it a foolish treatise, there will be at least this comfort left us—that if it was not very deep, neither was it very long.

Section II.

Democratic And Autocratic Theology

$\mathcal{W}$e distinguish theology democratic—theology growing from what is common and undisputed in the mind and life of man, from theology autocratic—the growth of singular minds, received of some by faith in a special divine illumination.

We dispute the revelations of no man's peculiar consciousness—a delicate topic; we but say, these were not revelations to us, but questionable hearsay, taken (if so) upon faith in his integrity. The experience of the abnormal individual is impertinent to the mass of men, whose experience is in a great measure common, each man's consciousness for the most part approving his fellow's. We deny not that in this normal mass there may be recipients of abnormal truth; yet we might question the sufficient purity of any finite mind to transmit to us that truth unsullied. "There is none good—no, not one," quoted the apostle Paul, to whom moderns attribute an infallibility which he denied to all men. All have strayed, saith he, and gone out of the way. Then from what human lip shall God breathe to us infallible abnormal truth? What John saw in Patmos was to him indisputable: but before what John avers to have seen should guide all other men, we think they may require some assurance that the revelator—going about in fantastic raiment, and eating locusts, was an honest man not only, but a sound man and sane. Many a wild eye has seen superhuman wonders. Many a man in delirium tremens has seen rats and reptiles which were never begotten of their kind: yet we must believe that the fellows of such men were unwise to forsake the judgments wherein they all agreed, to assume the madman infallible, and take him for a guide. His facts are improbable, impracticable and singular; they are not to be used if common facts shall be found competent.

We learn as we live that men are cut out upon an old pattern; no two are exactly alike perhaps, yet there is an old standard, both of mind and body, which contains the general race, and holds them amenable to the same laws. Most men can add one column of figures mentally, while few can add three columns at once; thus are we near together. So are there standard sympathies and sentiments: a thousand men, while they will agree that black is black, will laugh at the same jest, and be wroth at the same indignities. We are brothers born. So are there certain laws of reason which men generally acknowledge and always use; and there are certain facts apparent in all human being, which the various sets and sorts of men confess to, under the tuition of experience in their peculiar callings, age after age, and which no man of credit denies.—What we mean by democratic theology is the aggregate conclusion from the common and admitted experience of man, by the common and admitted laws of reason, as to the nature of divinity, the necessities of nature, and the course and policy of life: and this conclusion must appeal to no other authority than the common sense of the men in whom our facts are born. We desire to show that, without aid from any revelation of peculiar consciousness, there is deducible, at least in this late age, a most hopeful, glorious theology from the common lot of man—a lesson from the ages gone before.

Section III.

The Authority Of Reason

*D*eath alone can wholly ratify any religion; yet we must live by reason, and in the hope or fear of reason we must die. We see with the eye, we hear with the ear, —so do we judge and speculate with reason upon the understanding. The eye never was superseded as the seer, nor the ear as the hearer—for with nought else can we see or hear; yet both may have misled us: neither shall reason lose its position as the final and supreme judge, although two men's reasons may disagree, and both be in error. Denying the authority of reason, who is it that denies? Is it not reason defaming itself? Though we condemn all ratiocination of the past, we are but commending our present reason the more. An unsound judge cannot presently give sound judgment against himself. A serpent may bolt a goat of thrice his weight: but until he can take his own tail in his mouth, swallow himself, and bodily disappear, shall reason be the arbiter of truth. (How strange that aught so plain should need to be repeated!)

Section IV.

The Motives Of All Theorists

$\mathcal{P}$erhaps the true religion has been hit upon; yet it might not continue, in the want of exterior confirmation. And still, as of old, the last words of the prophet who believes himself a prophet shall echo the mournful cry of Jesus, "My God, my God, why hast thou forsaken me?"—Why did all earth's theorists preach and write? Did they believe that "they were the people, and wisdom would die with them?" Nay—behind the eye of the prophet the brain ached with labor. The theorists of to-day are the theorists of two thousand years ago. Those wrote as these do—not more to convince others than to make the concurrence of others convince them. Are they crowned? and is the crown refreshing?—not more for its honor than for that it comforts and conceals the baldness of their brows. Never a prophet comprehended the infinite; never a prophet held through age the opinions of his youth: rather shall we hold that all theology has been the varying convictions of men who often shifted their point of vision, and held their last opinions less confidently than they did their first. For why?—They had a lingering faith in the democratic mind. The traveller in lands where man never trod before—where the glories of nature lure him on in ecstacy, would fain tear up every shrub and flower, and bring them, with the birds all stuffed and the landscapes painted, to the land of his birth, that his own admiration may be approved by the praise of his fellows. The child scarcely looks at his new-found wonder till he runs for sympathy in the admiration of his peers. Then let the bold author affect to despise the world that denies him: he is not strengthened by foreign distrust. Let every man boast that nine out of ten are fools, and himself is a tenth man,—let him change a hundred times, and still insist that he is right at last,—yet only the sympathy of others can pacify his conviction. He finds himself a monster when none will agree with him; and he cannot lie down to die in peace, saying, "I alone of all God's creatures know the truth of God."

Section V.

The Burden Of Theology

*T*he burden of all theology has been to find the reason of pain in the present life, and to find hope in a life that shall be joyful, through the unwavering love of God. Theology for the most part, making much of the responsibility, and somewhat of the power of man, will have him win joy through duty, on peril of remediless woe. Our theology, making nothing of the power or responsibility of man, will find God making him continually wiser and freer, whether he seek vice or virtue. It will find God in boundless and unceasing love making man as happy as man himself could do with omnipotence. It will find that there is no sigh of the heart nor quiver of the lip that God would not hinder were it possible. It will find that the finite, now and forever, must have its trouble; but that no joy shall escape us which omnipotence can compass in our behalf. It will find man's highest earthly hopes to be courage, pride, health, knowledge, reason and charity,—and his highest hope for all time eternal progression towards an unattainable perfection of wisdom and serenity.

From the first recorded times man's ignorance of

the future has clothed God with terror, and knotted his brows with admonition. Yet all ages have said God is good; there is an ingenuity, and a beauty, a utility, a variety, a mitigation, a compensation in all nature, which men have indeed confessed, but partially—for the old question returns, Why are we not continually happy?— and even if such is God that we might be happy if we would, why have we not that wise disposition? Between these two facts: that we injure ourselves in part, and that God is good in nature, and especially to all those creatures wanting in man's high and seemly responsible intelligence, there has arisen a morality in our notions of action which has made us fear God as the master rather than love him as the lover of our race.

Moderns have found much in the Christian Scriptures (especially those written by the apostle Paul) to relieve this terror of God and the future. It is not our purpose to specially deny or coincide with any Scripture. But we think we shall not state amiss the orthodox interpretation of that which is written when we say that thereby the pains, cares, and sorrows of the world find no reason but God's will: He may do what he will with his own: in the sweat of his face, as the result of his sin, is man condemned to labor and to suffer, and for this reason solely. No kindly promise, in plain words of good assurance, is found to warn him that for all he suffers he shall be repaid with interest,—or to admonish him that all evil is for good.

Some speculators upon providence have made logic

serve for the assurance of God's love. They have said, It is the office of reason first to acknowledge that infinite wisdom will choose the best possible of systems; thereafter reason should study to reconcile itself to the system, rather than the system to itself. Perhaps this were a good method, were there not a better. We are slow to admit such tremendous premises. Let man see that the universe is working as he would prefer that it should work, and then man will see himself blessed, and will acknowledge the divine wisdom. He thinks God could make all men continually happy if he would, and therefore he does not find God as benevolent as himself. But if we can find that all things are for the best, not only in the light of divine but of human wisdom, were it not a blessed discovery? Answer, ye polished lines of the famous essays which deprecate the apparent difference in our mortal fortunes! It is not the justice of our ills that troubles us so much,—we are not badly perplexed that God should afflict us for our own wilfulness—and we feel that we may thank ourselves for so many of our troubles that the remainder thrown in would scarcely make the balance kick the beam—but it is the good of the whole method that puzzles us. We would question the benevolence that allows one folly on any account whatsoever,—which allows us to suffer for the sins of our ancestors, and allows many a thing to trouble us which neither we nor our ancestors have known how to point towards hope in the future. Life and its calamities we could endure for their own sake, if we saw any love of God in them; but if our

23

evil comes only from the wanton will of a despot, only woe, terror, and judgment can fill the gloomy passages of death.

These are the difficulties, dear reader. And now we shall presume to promise that if you will follow us closely to the end of our little volume, we shall at last defy you in the name of reason to change an atom of the universe, theoretically to fear death, or to murmur at your lot.

Section VI.

Concerning "The Beginning"

$\mathcal{W}$e who began look back for a beginning of all things. But if we will accept an eternal future, we must acknowledge the eternal past equally inevitable. The mind will not consent that space should have its limits, nor that time should end. Yet all creeds speak of The Beginning. Man will not leave unnamed the inconceivable, nor accept a destiny save toward something final. He seeks a place of eternal rest. He clothes his immortality with visible and definite flesh; he builds him an ethereal but tangible heaven; and with an old and fond idolatry he embodies his God. Do we condemn the pagan when he helps his worship with a graven image, while we strive to worship a God whom our imagination can contain? We are of one flesh with the pagan, and like him we would belittle all things to the measure of our comprehension. Yet we know, as he does, that this is not our proper method. And if we would come into intellectual peace we must let up the panting soul, and let her struggle with all indisputable truth. Fear not! for all is well. Fear not, though yours be an eternity with one end; it is an eternity nevertheless. Fear not for the tender sympathy of God, though he be impersonal. Fear not, though you should never attain one glimpse of the Almighty Friend, nor attain one moment's independent power; your power is in better hands—and His smile is greater than that the eye can see it. Tear away bravely the frightful background that fear has painted in life's picture, and send your gaze out unobstructed through the blue of eternal time.

Section VII.

Proofs Of God's Existence Impossible, &c.

Could we have proof of God's existence, there were no God worthy to be proved. Proof shifts its object into other essence, or other truth: but that which is infinite cannot be shifted to aught that is within our capacity. Incomprehensible as eternity, against what background shall our God stand relieved? Say space is filled, and time is filled, and we are a portion of that filling; how shall a part contain the whole?—how shall that which cannot be compassed be known, whether it be entirely proved or not? The poet cannot teach his poetry to a stone; nor can God condense his being to a picture in our souls; he were not God, nor we men. Yet God is in us, the assurance of his presence, whose majesty is the birth of reason. He is not afar, that we should see him. He is in the light of the eye, and in the object that it shines on. He is not a curiosity, a member of a species, or a thing to be represented by any device. He is the One—the original—the all in all. All creeds acknowledge him. His name needs no interpreter when they say "God created." Boundless and incomprehensible, yet indisputable, the key of

27

all mystery, without form, without centre or circumference, beginning or end, the life, space, and atmosphere wherein all being dwells, words were not made to present him; we cannot show him to another, nor another to us; yet in the human soul he has said immemorially, "I am! and there is none beside me!"

It is queried whether God is self-conscious.—If the heavens should burst in thunder and say *aye!* what were we the wiser? We cannot conceive universal consciousness; we cannot receive an answer though it were given. Think not because our language contains the word *universal* that the word must convey to us an idea. It is but the symbol of an inconceivable thought, useful to the finitude of the soul when it would acknowledge a greater than itself.

We delight to fancy a lone and glorious self-love in the Almighty; yet from this method has grown some of the worst of our theological discourse. It has made God in man's image. It has invested him with error, confusion, repentance, and worse than all, anger. It has made folly, sin; it has made policy, duty; it has made pain a judgment and a punishment; it has given to God all the frailties of man, and made man confound himself in efforts to prove—made him stultify himself in professions of faith in proof—that *justice* is lashing us solely for having opposed the will and thwarted the wishes of "the judge of all the earth." But from this conceit of God in man's image, bad though it be, worse conclusions are drawn than analogy will sanction. Will our heavenly father torture a child eternally for an offence at which his earthly father will but take him a box on the ear? We trace man's cruelty to his weakness—to envy, excess, disease; but all things must obey the will and subserve the purpose of the Almighty, and fear, envy, disappointment cannot ruffle his brow. Even man is noble, generous and forgiving. Place a human life in jeopardy, and many lives will be risked to save it. Friend or foe, be a man fallen, he is the brother of the human race. Scarce a man living would torture his enemy's dog for two days together; and shall He be believed to damn a man—He in whose image man was made?

Section VIII.

The Only Premise, One God

The only premise of our reasoning is, THAT THERE IS BUT ONE GOD, OR PERFECT BEING.—That there is one at all, according to human notions of perfection, can appear only at last, when we have vindicated his benevolence: but that there can be but one, if any there be at all, is a sentiment readily espoused by most men, and approved by the intelligent of all ages. The importance of this doctrine, though few of these days will contradict it, compels us to some brief mention of ancient books and men, whereby it may appear that this truth is not one of sectarian discovery or adoption.

It is the assumed policy of a class of theologians to encourage a saying which the masses have neither curiosity nor learning to dispute, that the Romans, Greeks, Brahmins, Persians, Chinese, and others were, in the absence of Christianity, idolators and worshippers of a plurality of gods.

Truly we cannot deny that in all nations there have been images of various features; nor shall we care to deny that there have been minds so base as to worship or pray to an image as a god. Nor shall we hesitate to agree

that there have been men in all nations who knew almost
nothing at all—a fact as clear to the intelligent of their
generation as is any fact to us of modern times. Nevertheless we detect in these animadversions a tendency to
exalt Christianity by dispraising the want of it, rather
than by praising the possession of it.—As for idolators,
we must be allowed to say that when man first dreams
of worship, be he never so barbarous, he is not an idolator. For before an image can be worshipped it must be
created: and he that hews the block cannot imagine that
the thing he is creating first created him, but he rather
believes that he is creating an image of that by which he
was himself created. Only time and teaching can make
this image a god to the mind of any man; for first its
origin must be forgotten.—We see there must be theists
before there can be idolators.—We can also observe that
men may very readily deceive themselves as to the intention of others, whose consciousness and motives they are
incompetent to determine. Every nation of the smallest
enlightenment has scorned the title of "idolator" as the
vilest reproach. No nation, nor book in any nation, did
ever inculcate idolatry essentially; but many peoples have
been thus reproached. Among these class all Catholics.
With what justice the reproach is cast we need but ask
Catholics themselves—for it is the intention, and not the
figure of the worship, which must determine its quality.

It is pleasing to us to look back over the records of the
earlier men of time, and to find that the wise of all ages
have been truly brothers in this doctrine of the unity of

God; and the more so because it is a doctrine which is attended with difficulties, when applied entirely to the destiny of man, which no record has come to us wholly explaining. We mean, chiefly, the difficulty of the origin of evil. Yet mark with what calm solemnity the first chapter of one of the oldest of books unfolds the doctrine of one God, in spite of evil:—"God is one: he has created all: it is a perfect sphere, without beginning or end . . .Thou shalt not seek to discover the nature and essence of the Eternal, nor by what laws he governs. Such an attempt would be vain, and criminal. . . . It is enough for thee to contemplate day and night his power, his wisdom, and his goodness, through his works."—This from the Shastah. Again:—"The sea enters the vessel that floats upon it; but time breaks the vessel, and the sea receives its own. And man is as a vessel, and God is as the sea; and the soul, God's power, returns to him who emitted it." This is not idolatry, nor polytheism.

From the foundation of the Roman empire no authentic book in the latin tongue has claimed that any other than Jupiter was "father of gods and men." "God most good, most great," was a title applied to Jove alone, to whom all other gods and spirits were but as saints in the calendar, or the fabulous representatives of ancient speculation. We shall submit a quotation which speaks for itself and all its age, from Maximus of Tyre, who flourished under the Antonines,—"Men have been so foolish as to give to God a human figure, because they have seen nothing superior to man; but it is only ridiculous to imagine with Homer that Jupiter, or the Supreme Deity, has black eye-brows and golden hair, which he cannot shake without making the heavens tremble! When men are questioned concerning the nature of Deity, their answers are all different. Yet notwithstanding this prodigious variety of opinions, you will find one and the same feeling throughout the earth, namely, that there is but one God, who is the father of all."—Fresh, fair and wise, as if it were written yesterday by the wisest critic of these latter days.

After times may condemn as polytheists all those who now worship the mystery of Three in One, far from suspicion of such a fate; and a petrified trilobite may pass for an idol of the nineteenth century, when this book, like Maximus', shall lie mouldering and unopened.—How ominous were the words of Cicero,—"The people may yet come to believe that these stones and pictures are the gods themselves!" Write *were* for *are*, and the prophecy is fulfilled.

Notice a little the wit of these ancients. "Here is money, my good woman—go buy you some geese and some gods therewith!" Horace makes a god say of himself, that his manufacturer doubted long whether to make his timber into a god or a bench.—"It is Jove," said Ovid, "whom we adore in the image of Jove."—Martial observes, "It is not the workman who makes the god, but he who adores it."—"The gods," saith Statius, "inhabit our minds and bosoms, and not the images of themselves." Is it not hard to conceive such a pitch of fancy as this worshipping idols, or, after the words of Maximus, worshipping a whole litter of gods? Every Greek and Roman capable of religious speculation knew full well that the inferior deities, the sons and daughters of heaven, earth, and hell, promiscuously, were but abbreviations of the wit and wisdom of the Homeric age—that they were virtues and vices personified. Very probably some of the illiterate, to whom a book was more than now a sealed and mysterious thing, adopted as literal the fables which the more educated cared not to explain to them. Hence the satire of the wit to an old woman, "Go buy you some geese and some gods!"

Even so the Egyptians, whose dwellings swarmed with embalmed cats, oxen and crocodiles, worshipped one only God, Knef, the father and master of the universe. Isis and Osiris were but children of the skies, no more liable to reproach than Gabriel and Michael, of orthodox repute. The Chinese have worshipped one God, Kien Tien, from time immemorial, without inferior gods,—the Emperor being sovereign pontiff, and viceroy of God.

Yet we must be careful not to give these ancients too much credit, for, like the moderns with rare exceptions, (by their favor) they have made God no better than a determined master, whose banner showed no insignia but the death's head and thigh-bones. Some of their philosophers, advancing into religious speculation, devised theories which were meant to account for evil in the world, while yet they hoped in the purity of the one

God. Thus we have, amongst others, the eternal conflict of two equal beings; a conflict in which the better of two eternal beings shall ultimately triumph; and a devil by permission, who shall work yet some definite period. Under the latter method we have sects making man himself more or less the principal in his own final destruction, we can hardly determine whether in spite of the Almighty, or by his permission, or by making Him the author of both good and evil. Among them all, we will bear the reproach of saying, there is no perfectly satisfactory theory. The philosophical minds of the earth have, for the most part, approved Father Lactantius, where, on the "Anger of God," chapter 13, he makes Epicurus speak as follows: "God can either take away evil from the world, and will not; or, being willing to do so, cannot; or he neither can nor will; or, lastly, he is both willing and able. If he is willing to remove evil, and cannot, he is not omnipotent. If he can remove it, but will not, he is not benevolent. If he neither can nor will remove it, he is neither all-powerful nor benevolent. Lastly, if he is both willing and able to annihilate evil, why does it exist?" The learned father answers himself in more modern prolixity, and we think with indifferent satisfaction, by the argument that man has power to choose the good,—and though he choose the evil, God stands unreproached. Few men reproach God with evil intention: conscience restrains them.

We have chiefly desired that it should appear the general conviction of the thoughtful that there is but one

God. That they could not account for evil was a conviction which came afterward. We can readily understand how this inability occasioned a proposition that there were powers under God, which created evil, leaving the one God pure; and we are encouraged the more to believe in one God, because in that belief alone can we give evil any rational account. So far from requiring another power to produce the evil of the world, in order to preserve the one God pure, to us the proof of his purity depends entirely on his solitary power.—Grant us but this: that all-knowledge must control all-power,—that all truth is one, and must rest in one omniscience,—in short, that there can be but one free, all-wise, almighty God, and then we shall declare that a single will and purpose are necessary to the harmony, safety and good of the universe,—and from this necessity will grow out others whereby the Gordian knot shall unravel without a stroke of the sword.

This, then, is our presumption—there is but one God. And now we say, the harmony of any supposable system requires the guidance of a single will and purpose. Partly for this reason men have believed in one God, taking the harmony of the world upon faith, though they saw it not clearly. Any power, independent of the first, can be operated only by a limited intelligence, and must run counter to the great and perfect purpose. For if it be permitted to act independently, it must either conform to, or diverge from that purpose; if it must invariably conform, it cannot be independent, being subservient by its inherent and unavoidable nature; (of this hereafter;) and if it shall invariably diverge, being independent, only disorder, confusion, and ruin can be the result. Here then we shall admit that whatever power or intelligence man may possess must, for his own good and the good of the system of which he is a part, be of an entirely subservient character. This is the moral to the fable of the Sphinx.

Section IX.

Interpretation Of Fables

$\mathcal{W}$e read in ancient fable that the Sphinx sat by the way-side, and propounded to every passer-by a riddle to this effect: What is that animal which in the morning goes upon four legs, at noon goes upon two legs, and at night goes upon three legs? If the traveller could answer truly, the Sphinx should be slain; if not, then the Sphinx would swallow him. The question is simple if we would merely suggest an animal that goes in this method: for man goes first on all four of his limbs in the morning of life,—at life's noon he is on his legs,—and in life's evening he steadies his two legs with a staff. It is said that Œdipus answered the riddle, whereat the enraged Sphinx threw herself into the sea. There are other tales, of various import, in regard to the Sphinx,—all of which are wanting in significance. We can but think that a soul more exalted than those which the authors of these tales possessed was the deviser of that most significant of images, whose meaning was hidden from the many.

The Sphinx is an idol, or symbol of God. It is the head and breast of man, on the body of a winged dog with lions' paws. It is an expression, by the highest earthly types, of intelligence, power, ubiquity, and integrity, through man, the wisest, the lion, the most formidable, the eagle, the swiftest, and the dog, the most faithful of the earth. It is the profoundest sculpture of the past, and in its solemn dignity is a fit companion to the winged globe of the Egyptian tombs. And he that devised this image was not so shallow as to illustrate therewith a riddle of so easy a solution as this of man on four legs, two legs, and three legs. Sustain the question, after this answer. Say, what is man? and then we have a riddle which comports with the original dignity of the image. The Sphinx, God, propounds the riddle of existence. To know this riddle is to know all things, to possess all power, and be the god of God—the master and destroyer of the Sphinx. Not to know it, is to be swallowed, contained, comprehended by, and subservient to, his being and his purpose. This is the moral: all things must be perfectly subservient, inferior to and dependent on God, or God and all harmony in nature must be broken up and destroyed. The Sphinx still lives, and the story of Œdipus is void of the true significance thereof.

The infinity of knowledge is the destruction of all Gods but one. Truth is one. Two omnisciences melt in one. Two omnipotences melt in one. There can be but one good universal, and good has no difference with itself. And as truth and power forbid a second God, harmony forbids a second independent will.

It will appear no reproach to omnipotence, that it cannot create nor tolerate a second God. On the contrary, the possibility of an equal forbids supremacy. We must not say that every supposition is a possibility with God. It is no reproach to perfection that it cannot be imperfect,—nor to supreme power that it cannot be controlled. And it may be that, though God be both omnipotent and benevolent, evil cannot be separated from the existence of man, because the perfection of the first intelligence insists on the imperfection of all others. And if the existence of man be better than no existence at all, God's benevolence shall suffer no reproach in man's creation, provided that we shall find this existence mitigated and compensated in every possible manner within the pale of this necessary inferiority and subservience.

We must observe here that the perfection of God insists on the imperfection of all other beings, not in any such sense that we should now say that he causes man to violate the laws which surround him; but we here say that man as an intelligent and active being must in his very nature exist in violation of the mode of perfect being, or the throne of God must slide into utter confusion: not so much that he must *do* wrong, but in his nature he must *be* wrong, or imperfect as an intelligence, beside the perfect standard, God. Doubtless we may find ample reasons for belief that a being, imperfect in itself, should necessarily show imperfection in its acts: but calling this mere probability, the first proposition is a certainty in itself. Man must have imperfect intelligence or he must have perfect power;—and as men are many, and God the controller must be one, there is no alternative but to submit to the imperfection of the many;—for to place one perfect man at the head of the universe could be no improvement, and no release from finitude of all the rest.

There appears a distinction between soul and aught else as respects perfection. Every thing is perfect or imperfect by the standard of its kind, by the fitness to its use, and the fulness of its growth. The perfection of God is not necessarily amenable to the soul's ideal. If we shall find God perfect, well; but even if we do not, eternity is before us, in which, by what ways we know not, God's perfection may yet shine through the clouds of tribulation into our imperfect understanding. The perfection of providence admitted, all things are in one sense perfect in the purpose of their being. Nevertheless a fragment of a cube is not a perfect cube; nor is a limited intelligence a perfect soul. The circle can be completed; the line cannot. There is a sense in which any body may be called a perfect body, while only God can be a perfect soul. A body may grow to the standard of its species, perfect of its kind. But the standard of ideal intelligence rises with intelligence itself, to God, to whom soul may never grow; nor can it reach the perfection of its kind, for this alone is of divine kindred: this alone declares its own imperfection in the want of infinite expansion.

Man's moral qualities, so called, are the result, not so much of mind's simple action as of its consciousness of action, and of self-speculation or contemplation. Free from this self-contemplation,—free from the knowledge of the infinite beyond him, the brute, (or man in his lowest condition,) may be supposed to be in a low grade of perfection. Food will always fat him, and, free from prophecy, hope, and metaphysical fear, with a full belly he is content. But when the mind passes on from mere formal action upon its body's wants to self-inspection, it discovers its imperfection as a merely fragmentary intelligence; it discovers itself as God in chains; and thenceforth the world seems darkened while it struggles to be free. This discovery awakens discontent, ambition, and metaphysical hope and fear: and although this knowledge is in truth an advance over man's former position, yet inasmuch as man hereby discovers that which is the occasion of all intellectual discontent, the advance has been counted to his disadvantage, and called a Fall, and a Curse.

It is one of the oldest theories in the world, that man was pure and happy as a brute, and that he fell by reason of forbidden knowledge. Afterward came the theory that through vice, error and misery, he should grow to *perfect* purity and happiness, through knowledge itself.

We read of human progress until man shall attain a perfect being. This we cannot understand. Shall he who knows little ever know all? Shall the finite comprehend the infinite?—a part the whole? As long as one secret lies beyond us, that secret is the key of the universe, and hangs at the girdle of the Almighty. We read of perfect being as a man, though not as God. This also we cannot understand. Is a fragment perfect, though it fit the block it fell from? Though man be a portion of a perfect system, filling his place perfectly, yet what is man? In those attributes which are his chief distinguishments—the powers of apprehension and will, he is of necessity imperfect, by any ideal standard of perfection. And the same necessity which has made him imperfect now must cover all grades of finite being, now and evermore.

It will be interesting to us to trace the speculations of the ancients, through their fables, upon this subject of the *fall by knowledge* of the human race. The fables of Prometheus, Tantalus, and the Fall of Man in the Brahmin Shastah, and in the Old Testament, are all very nearly similar in their doctrine and purpose. Let us look first at the story of Prometheus.

The story goes that Prometheus, a man, stole fire from heaven to inform and enlighten a man of clay whom he had made. As a retribution for this theft, Jove ordered Vulcan to forge a box, which he filled with all evils, first putting hope in the bottom, and sent it by the hands of Pandora to Prometheus. The latter, suspicious of the contents, handed it to his brother Epimetheus, who opened it. Hereupon the evils flew out of the box abroad into the world; and Epimetheus closed timely the cover over hope, which alone remained in the box. Prometheus was then chained upon a rocky mountain, where an eagle daily came and feasted on his vitals, which daily grew again. Time passed, and ultimately Jupiter sent Hercules to slay the eagle, and set Prometheus at liberty.

The name, Prometheus, is derived from a Greek word, signifying foresight, providence, or speculation.

He is represented as man exalting man to the possession of more heavenly powers, by means of effort, or
foresight, or speculation, as you please. The man of
clay receiving the heavenly light through the agency of
man, represents the supposed promotion of man from
the mere brute consciousness—the clay-soul, to the soul
self-contemplative, whereby he discovers that there is an
infinite above and around his finite being, and whereby
he aspires after the perfect. The consequence, to the mass
of men, was all the evil and trouble since come upon
them,—whether as a punishment, or as an alleviation,
does not explicitly appear, save from the assertion that
hope still remained in the hands of man,—and that it
came as the very foundation of the whole parcel of his
evils. Prometheus—the God in man which would exalt
him—the speculative spirit, thenceforth finds itself in finite bonds, while the eagle of ambition (or the vulture
of conscience, as you will,) gnaws at his vitals, which
daily grow, or rather nightly grow, again. That is, the
animal nature, of its own force, and reacting tendency,
defies the unattained infinite, and keeps him still alive.
In the true spirit of the fable, Prometheus still is bound,
and the eagle gnaws him still. But another and a baser
hand has marred the fable, in the view of finishing that
which never can be finished, and added the conclusion
that Hercules, or the perfection of the physical man, fi-
nally slew or shall slay the longing, hungry curiosity and
ambition of the soul, and set it at perfect liberty.

Let us look at another fable. Tantalus, although a son

of Jove, was a speculator in theology. He invited all the gods to his table, and even sacrificed and served thereon his own son, that he might discover somewhat concerning their divinity. But the gods smelled his design, and would not eat of his repast, but took Tantalus and fixed him in the midst of the waves, where he is tormented nevertheless with a thirst which he cannot allay.

If we shall credit some expositors, this fable represents the condition of a miser, who, in the midst of plenty, is in continual want. But Ovid declares that the crime of Tantalus was discovering the secrets of the gods to men.

This is the old story repeated,—the elevation of man to too much knowledge; and the "punishment" is that, in the midst of Deity and truth, he thirsts forever after the ocean which he cannot compass. As soon as man discovers the infinite about him,—as soon as he knows so much as that he knows nothing of first principles,—the secrets of the gods, the thirst after the knowledge of life begins: and it must endure while only God is perfect in intelligence and power. Tantalus will never die, nor will Prometheus be unbound.

But older and profounder than Tantalus or Prometheus is the fable proper of the Fall of Man, though the substance is much the same. The stolen light from heaven, and the box of evils consequent thereon,—and the stolen fruit of the tree of the knowledge of good and evil, and the thorns and thistles consequent thereon, bespeak a common purpose and a common origin. The substance of the supposed original lies between the fourth verse of the second chapter of Genesis and the last of chapter third.

"And out of the ground made the Lord God to grow every tree that is pleasant to the sight and good for food: the tree of life also, in the midst of the garden, and the tree of knowledge of good and evil. . . . . And the Lord God commanded the man, saying, Of every tree of the garden thou mayst freely eat: but of the tree of the knowledge of good and evil, thou shalt not eat of it; for in the day that thou eatest thereof thou shalt surely die. . . . The woman took of the fruit, and gave also to the man. . . . And the eyes of them both were opened, and they knew that they were naked. . . . And they hid themselves. . . . And the Lord God called unto Adam. . . . And the man said, I was afraid because I was naked, and I hid myself. And He said, Who told thee that thou wast naked? Hast thou eaten of the tree? . . . . And unto the man he said, *Cursed is the ground* for thy sake: in sorrow shalt thou eat of it all the days of thy life. Thorns also, and thistles shall it bring forth. . . . In the sweat of thy face shalt thou eat bread all the days of thy life. . . . And the Lord God said, Behold, the man has become as one of us, to know good and evil: and now, lest he put forth his hand, and take also of the tree of life, and eat and live forever, therefore the Lord God sent him forth from the garden of Eden to till the ground from whence he was taken. So he drove out the man: and he placed at the East of the garden of Eden cherubims, and a flaming sword which turned every way, to keep the way of the tree of life."

The inculcation plainly is that man, in some distant era, was a thinking, but not self-contemplative being, even as the chiefest of all animals, and thus was pure, because he knew not impurity; he was naked, but was not ashamed; for only the consciousness of a higher being, or higher standard, can make us ashamed, or conscience-stricken. But with advancing knowledge he came to see himself in the light of a fragmentary intelligence—a portion of a perfect soul; and awed by the thought of that perfection of which he had so little—hearing the voice, and feeling the presence of God in all the world of beauty, he was ashamed and afraid. This sense of nakedness is the first result of his knowledge of good and evil—the infinite and the finite. "Who told thee that thou wast naked? Hast thou eaten," &c.—Who waked thee from the soul conscious to the soul self-conscious? Thou hast obtained the forbidden knowledge.

The fault we find with all these fables is, that there is no clear assurance whether the evils which came of this advancement to knowledge as of the gods were in truth a punishment or an alleviation. The dullest eye must see that knowledge as of the gods, even though forbidden knowledge, must afford man some compensation, and do him some good. Therefore in the fable, God no where curses man; but rather, "cursed is the ground for thy sake." Yet there is no reason given for this cursing of the ground, except God's will. So in the fable of Prometheus, hope is still left in the parcel of our evils; but the rationale of that hope is left for the reader to prescribe.—Death was assured of the Lord God as the result of this forbidden knowledge. Many have doubted whether death was not welcome to an old man; and we cannot judge whether this was meant as a curse or a blessing. Certain we are that no man yet has complained to us that death has hurt him.—We can readily conceive that man, after he had discovered the comparative extent of his intelligence, would have concluded that the directest mode of increasing it was by death: he would have embraced death with rapture. Then why does the fable place the tree of life (which can mean only death) behind a terror which "turns every way," and frightens man from its approach? We have our reason: it is because no advance can satisfy man's curiosity; and there are excellent reasons why man should stay on the earth for a time. The terror of death is of benefit to him. But it is not clear in the fable whether this terror was a blessing or a curse. And we say of all these fables together, they are misty and oracular, and little to our purpose. Had their authors been competent to the subject, we had not needed now to have questioned their intention.—We speak of the fables as we find them, believing that time has altered them. We love to think that far in the forgotten past some lone and lofty genius saw the reason of the cursing of the ground, and saw with a prophet's vision those windings of the human race which should make that reason the common property of mankind.

Here, then, we indicate the primal necessity of evil in the world. The harmony or perfection of the universe

requiring the guidance of a single will and perfect intelligence, all other intellectual beings must necessarily be
fractional and subservient, and incapable of intellectual
perfection: and by so much as they are made greater, and
more clearly see or believe in the infinite Perfect, by so
much the more will the lesser require divertisement from
its longing curiosity, fear, and envy of the necessarily
despotic, though benevolent First. The rationale of this
divertisement will be the theory of what are called evils
in the world, —but which we shall call the alleviations
of the only misfortune of all finite beings, namely, the
eternal necessity of the eternal imperfection of every intelligent being but one, in order to the greatest happiness
and harmony of all.

Section X.

Sundry Inferences
—The Heaven Of Progression

*B*efore advancing, it will be to our pleasure and profit to draw sundry inferences from the foregoing, which may throw some little light both before and behind us,— inferences concerning the immortality of the soul.

We risk little in saying that most theology stops at the gates of heaven. The theory of the soul's eternity after death (supposing it immortal) is not, until recently, a subject of practiced thought. To "get to heaven" is to be happy, and there theology rests. Yet it must be obvious that the soul, any where, will be confined by certain eternal necessities. It is not our purpose here to argue for or against the immortality of the soul: we shall leave this as a deduction from our treatise, and speak briefly here of the necessary nature of that immortality, wherever or whenever supposed.

In what sense the soul is distinct from God in its being—how we can live through his life, in a being of which he is the only and constant light, it is vain to conjecture. And if we cannot analyze the divine connection now, it is equally vain to conjecture how we may dwell in any other essence more rationally. We easily conceive ourselves invested in bodies or spheres of palpitating, ethereal lightness, which may fly, at will, around the pendant world; yet the sense in which we were independent of God's consciousness in our own would be as mysterious as now. However we exist, doubtless we shall feed only upon his bounty, and shall never inspire ourselves.

The first thought we wish to urge is the eternal finitude of the soul. If the finite cannot comprehend the infinite now, no progress can ever bring it nearer to that comprehension. Nothing that God has created can ever behold him, nor ever learn the secret force of its existence. No angel, nor saint, nor prophet was ever admitted to the council of God. We muse of departed spirits— we think the dead have found out something. Truly they have,—but not all they expected. They have not found out the Almighty unto perfection. They dreamed, perhaps, that death would bring them into some clear being which should teach them the mystery of life. But doubt not, as they bloom up through the youth of their second life, they will begin to learn that death is still ahead— death, mystery and God. "Thou shalt surely die"—not once only, but a thousand thousand times. If we shall live again, doubt not that we shall die again: wherever there is finite life, death is the consequent. But let this pass. Death cannot be an infinite advance. The second life is at no such vast remove from the first, either in the height of the grade or the character of the consciousness

thereof. Doubt not that there are theories and speculations in the second life, as to the nature of the third;
and there are legends and revelations also, both real and
deceptive, even as here. We shall enter that state belated,
even as we did this. A pretentious past will be behind us,
to rebuke and censure our parvenue theology. But our
answer is recorded: We may change forever, but we cannot know the end. Death can wake us to none but the
bottomless, the incomprehensible life. Yon starry host,
whose golden harps are humming far within the bosom
of God, have not yet read their destiny, nor his purpose.
And something whispers us, that though they be older,
and higher, and brighter than we are, God loves us as
tenderly as them. The brave, true heart on earth is nobler than the learned head; and we doubt not that pale
John Huss, though deceived and headstrong, shall yet for
the brave and gentle heart within him shine brighter in
heaven than Copernicus and Newton, with constellations sparkling on their heads.

And with the finitude of intellect will go, undoubtedly, the imperfect heart and purpose. We must err in
the head, though the heart were pure; and therefore folly
will find us, though at the foot of the throne. Say you
there is a place or a time "where the wicked cease from
troubling, and the weary are at rest?" Yet who are the
wicked? "There is none good—no, not one!" Who shall
sunder the absolute good from the absolute evil, where all
are comparatively imperfect by the sole standard, God? It
will ever be so, even in "heaven." As long as we are fi-

nite, the nearest joy will shine the brightest. We will rob
the future for the present. None are utterly exempt: and
ever as now, (and why not?) the bad man, and the good
man, or the man less bad, shall tread the same plane.

To us this thought reflects with force upon the more
difficult features of modern spiritualism. The most
popular objections to these manifestations are their fre-
quent error and very common folly and pretension. To
us this blundering is one of the most reliable confirma-
tions of the reality of spiritual intercourse. It comports
with this doctrine that death is no infinite advance—that
the dead have not learned every thing. And if the reader
can but believe that there are some liars, some knaves,
and some fools in the second life, as well as in the first,
these dark answers, plain deceptions, and driveling bom-
bast will seem less inconsistent with the reputed grav-
ity of death. Strip death of its vagaries, make it a plain
matter,—say that the dead man lives on,—and then it
will not be expected that a dead fool is wiser than a living sage, nor a dead knave more honest than a dying
martyr. Perhaps if spirits have communicated recently
with men, some spirit who has called himself Benjamin
Franklin has been a rogue: for Benjamin Franklin was
a cautious man, too wise to commit himself on earth
without most conclusive evidence,—which perhaps he
has not yet found to his satisfaction. You will not expect
to find the Emperor of France devoting his energies to
the training of an obscure school in the Parisian suburbs?
Then why should we expect Gallileo to return, to as-

sure us that his calculations were correct? The dead have their equals to converse with; why should they desire to teach us underlings? That a grandmother of an affectionate nature should return, recently dead, to console a relative in whom she had ever taken more interest than in metaphysical progression, is not inconsistent; nor is it outrageous to propose that a newly-buried Dutchman should as yet deliver an indifferent message to the Chinese: but to propose that a born villain—a lecherous, treacherous, and bloody knave, should, in a week after his decease, have grown as benevolent as Howard, as calm as Washington, as wise as Shakspeare, and as pure as him whose holy life has named him the Saviour of men, would seem very inconsistent and unreasonable, even though all souls are similar, and varied by the body in effects. It is but rational, that spirits should require time, in order to form just opinions of the second life. Men may look well about them, and seek for the truth as it is in this world, and they will find plenty ready to contradict them, even to their face. Let us not be disgusted then if spirits should differ in their reports,—or if some of them should lie occasionally,—or if there is many a thing that we should like to know which the second life at its best is unable to tell us. Neither be discouraged if spiritual intercourse should some day be a well-proved delusion, or if its facts prove to be facts of an unhealthy origin. There is a blessed religion which asks no revelation out of the common course of life. And lest we shall have grown a little tiresome and unpromising, we shall offer here an encouraging word or two which otherwise had been as well said later.

Will the reader say to himself, this is a startling, hopeless basis of joy—this belief in an unattainable perfection, and a destiny without a goal or an end? Nay, thou shalt live to rejoice in this truth as in no other, that thy destiny shall have no end; and the starry path, for itself alone, shall be prouder and brighter than the porch of fancy's fairest temple, or the prize of any supposable goal. We know the good earth sits fast. We dig through her shifting sands, and reaching the solid rock, we build as for eternity. All things seem set and appointed: we have our youth, then manhood, then gray hairs, and death is the end of all; the course is plain; the end is sure: therefore it is that we are repulsed from thought of a life that cannot pause, nor rest, nor attain an end. But, reader, there is no creed on earth but inculcates the same bottomless infinite. The sentiment is old,—it is almost universal, although its consequents may be apparent only to the thoughtful. It is the secret to every puzzle, the key to every fable under the sun. As we grow old in the ways and wisdom of the world—as we begin to learn that the joys we compass slip from our fruition like water from the lips of Tantalus, we shall learn to set our affections on things infinitely above us, and to rejoice in the only consolation of our vast ambition—that there is no final, ultimate ideal of which we might grow weary.

We know the Heaven of man's sensual dreams. There is golden, glorious light there, and music, as the forest pines were strung to the arch of the rainbow, and thrilled by exhilarating winds—winds that remember the brown eternities of the slumberous land of Egypt, and the marbles wrecked in Asia,—winds that blow over the cedars of Lebanon and the groves of Arabia, and bear their enchanting legends through the strings. He shall have joy in a swift moving and ethereal nature; he shall pace the golden streets, and look out from the crystal battlements of the City of God; and the stars shall sing again to the roses of nature, as through the dews of the world's first morning. But what of God the while, my brother?— what of the infinite and the eternal? Think you to loiter on the same flowery banks, and listen to the purling of the same silver streams, forever? Where is that everhungry Soul which even now—smothered in flesh until it can dote upon the jingle of a rhyme, can long for the harmonies of universal law, and wonder how free, how brave, how happy it may ever grow? Where is the wit that conceived of the ambition of Lucifer, and the treason of Uriel? Is it content? We too can see a day when purer life and purpose may vanquish many of our ills,—when the elements may know us as a friend,—when we may make acquaintance at will with every tribe and science of our sphere,—yea, when all that the race now knows to covet may be gained: but in this material and definite outline does the hope of Heaven end? Nay—it does not here begin. Not in the hope of a blessed abode, in music, and light, and dreams,—not in the hope of eternal rest, by houris fanned,—but in the hope of the glory of God—

in the hope of eternal advancement,—yea, even in the knowledge that there is no home, nor stay, nor station on the wild, bright way we know not whither, we shall spurn these heavens of the dull imagination. From the colonnades and temples in gardens elysian, where blooms of amaranth shade the lamb and the lion, and fancy hears the foot-falls of the loftiest of time, past thrones, princi-palities, and constellations,—past crowns whose jewels win the lifted eyes of Gabriel and Michael, up through laws and harmonies which it hath not entered into the heart of man nor angel to conceive—which are to music as is music to the grating of a dungeon hinge, shall rise the flying soul,—and the blessed air shall echo to her shouting, far o'er the lost ideals of the world, "thanksgiv-ing! thanksgiving to the Lord God Almighty, who calls and calls us through the universe of glory!"

Section XI.

"Metaphysics"

*H*aving now hinted at certain necessities of all being, it becomes our pleasant task to show that, these necessities being admitted, God is doing all for us that we can suggest in our own behalf,—in truth, that reason promises us, through Him, all things but his throne. Assuming now that there can be but one Perfect Being, the harmony of whose reign insists on the eternal docility of all others who shall be favored with existence in the system, we shall find that all our evils are most beautifully good. We shall find that there is no sin against God, nor punishment as such, nor divine wrath in the world—but that all is in love and harmony, and good will to men.

But as we advance to this exposition, the world confronts us with a mountain of metaphysics concerning the will, and the responsibility of man. Not content that the term *evil* should be synonymous with *pain*, or that which produces it, and that *good* should be synonymous with *joy* and its efficients, all time considered—these being in their conceit very low and brutish admissions—men have conceived a notion of a higher good than pleasure, and a notion that evil is not so great in the pain that comes of it as in the "sin" of violating high law—especially the Scriptural law. Violation of the written law is considered sin in an entirely different sense from that of violation of the unwritten laws. The unwritten laws are of temporal, while the written laws are of eternal consequence. We might go so far as to say that some austere minds delight in setting the two orders of law in antagonism, and purposely violating the latter as the height of subservience to the former. With these ascetics, to steal a gill of aqua-fortis were a sin; to drink a gill of aqua-fortis were but folly: the first act has purely moral, the last has purely physical consequences; the first is a case for conscience, while a man may violate the laws of health, and be a timid and nerveless drone with excellent virtue. There is a blending of truth and falsehood, of wisdom and folly in their system of religion, from a misapprehension of the true policy of virtue, and the true folly of sin. We shall find that in the right conception of the matter all violations of law are equally immoral; that there is no greater good than pleasure, and that there is no right above expediency.

It would seem that an unprejudiced mind could detect no lack of dignity in any creed that promised its votaries eternal pleasure. But a different sentiment prevails in many pure and well meaning minds,—a sentiment which separates purity and pleasure, and puts the latter eternally subservient to the former,—so that not even suffering in this world in order to [gain] happiness in the next is conscientious; a truly good soul seeks heaven not for its pleasure, but to comply with God's requirement, which were equally binding whether pain or pleasure were the final result. We think few would go so far as to say they should serve God though they were to be damned for it, but a notion prevails of which this is a legitimate inference. Pardon us when we say this notion is a most transparent delusion, growing from a misapprehension of the genius of God's providence. You say God will punish eternally the most of us,—you say he is punishing us now,—you say there is evil in the world which doubtless God might remove should he neglect to be just,—you say this is a world of sin and sorrow,—all for the sake of right and divine glory—there is no sense in providence but for these—therefore Right is above the measure of our base expediency. But if we shall find God unerringly and unceasingly good—find that all our pains and sorrows are the only means of human happiness—find that although pain follows error, both were in mercy,—find in short that God's severity is in love to us, then the stern Right which would eternally defy happiness will be but the synonym of divine expediency, the father and the friend of Pleasure. Then sin will be folly, but nothing worse; then virtue will be policy, and nothing better; then pain will be the sum of all evils, and joy will be the holiest thing in the heavens above, or in the earth beneath; then the majesty of the Law will be the majesty of our suffering nature, and that right which does no being good will fly wild in the universe, unowned of God or man.

We know that glory of a good deed which lives independent of all reward: we know that the generous heart of man may be roused into passion whence it will leap into the jaws of death, yea, or damnation, defying time and flood and fire, and all of mad or terrible that words can utter or imagination grasp; we know that the royal soul can for time or eternity prefer another to itself, in a course of lofty virtue which shall never consult its own welfare;—but it cannot deprive itself of the greatness which dictates and rewards the sacrifice; it cannot so be forgotten of our God, but the self-good which it neglects shall be God's especial care.

"The exceeding sinfulness of sin" is a conception designed to justify an eternal punishment. The vastness of our iniquity being not too well apparent in the iniquity itself, it is aggravated by the exaltation of "The Law." The orthodox sentiment of Sin finds its origin, not so much in the apparent discord of violated law, as in the consciousness of such independence of any supposable Lawgiver as allows us to violate any supposable divine law as much in our own freedom as we break the laws of men—for which last violation we account ourselves justly punished. Man must be free of God and the world in his acts, or he cannot be justly punished of God therefor. Many men satisfy themselves that they are not free of either God or the world, and, doubting not that God is just, insist that man never shall be punished. Meantime they find that man has much pain and trouble here, whether it be punishment or not. It will be necessary for us to look into the question of man's Free Agency.

That God does reign, in the armies of heaven and among the inhabitants of the earth,—that there is none that spake and it came to pass, and the Lord commanded it not,—that the world in every atom, and the soul in every thought is as God would have it, is a dictate of even the common decency of reverence. All men have at some time confessed it, and none can assure us how it might be otherwise. At the same time every man feels a sufficient independence of God that he may attempt to insult and defy him, and disobey his laws. We feel that we may be justly commanded of God, and are at liberty to obey. We feel that if we stood on the threshold of heaven, invited to enter, and should declare with tears in our eyes that we could not enter until God should give us a disposition so to do, the devil himself, with all his reputed sophistry, could not outmatch our effrontery. We feel that God may require our good will, however we obtain it.

But few minds are so shallow as to attempt, in these days, to reconcile with human notions of justice the assertion that God requires of man the will which He alone can give. Men deny the validity of that instinct which feels independent of God. If one man controls the consciousness of another, either with drugs or any force whatsoever, common justice forbids that the second should be responsible to the first for word or deed. His consciousness of individual liberty is a delusion. Men see that God has at least such control over them, and they repudiate their alleged responsibility.

Much argument has been put forth to show that God could make a being independent of himself, and therefore responsible to him. But sad were our fate if any but God held independent power; and reason scouts the proposition for its own absurdity. For every being, independent or otherwise, created or uncreated, finds itself, in the mere fact of being, individualized, with a definite and peculiar nature; and whether it act, or think, or merely exist, it must act, or think, or exist in this nature. However free to act this nature, it is not free to forsake it; and whether or not motives in the outer world may bias its volition or its direction, it must find in itself if not elsewhere the reason of its peculiar course. Not God himself can be supposed to transcend his nature; nor can any being that he has created: only the forced positions of an erroneous system ever could have driven men to the invention of a free will—free of the world, free of its creator, and free of its own construction, without bounds or definition.

The consciousness of freedom from God, (of which we shall see a beautiful utility hereafter,) is properly a consciousness of the original or unself-contemplative man who has not discovered the meaning of divinity, and is refuted by reason in the advancement of humanity—reason based upon experience. We find that men have each a peculiar nature, which no single volition can alter, whatever time and custom may accomplish. Our friend is usually, "the same old sixpence," though years have passed. Perhaps his sentiments have changed; but

the character or basis of the man supports the new sentiments with much the same force as it did the old. That
which the polemics call moral inability is as determined
as any inability physical. Motives cannot be resisted,—
which means but this—the mind and not the motive is
the actor, and the mind can act only according to its nature. A man may walk a plank that lies on the earth, with
coolness and with ease: but lift that plank a hundred feet
in the air, and although it is not physically more difficult
than before, he may be unable to keep his feet upon it.
He has not the *mind*, which only nature or long practice
can bestow. So is it with the path of virtue: high, narrow, apparently impracticable, only the cool head and
the brave heart, even with the best of training, can keep
a man therein—nor did God ever design or wish them
to. A man who faints at the presence of a bugbear cannot
die a martyr to a principle. An inexperienced lout cannot fix the lightning-rod on a slim and lofty steeple, nor
stand unswerving on the summit of Mount Blanc. Most
men will fall from such heights as surely as if they were
stricken with a club. He that will deny it, let him mount
and try it.

Still the fact remains, that God does give law, and
does visit with pain the violation thereof, whether or
not he causes that violation. He has said to man's flesh,
Beware of fire! and he that touches fire is burnt. Nor
were it inconsistent to suppose law to be imposed upon
any state of human life hereafter, and its violation visited
with similar reward.—The inconsistency of the visita-

tion will depend entirely on its objects and results, even as here. You will say, "This is not justice—to give us our will, and punish us therefor."—No, it is not justice, but benevolence. Were the penalty eternal pain, surely it were neither justice nor benevolence: but if the penalty is of limited extent, and beneficial to the recipient, perchance the hand that guides us both to err and to suffer will be for ever blessed; and that which appears punishment now may be providence in reality.

We think the chief difficulty, which has made conclusions unsatisfactory to a large and increasing class of men, is a misunderstanding of justice, and a confusion of the notions of divine and human justice—of right which is right by law, and right wherein both law and its violation find their expediency.

The original of the justice of nature is revenge—an instinct of all flesh, which finds its expression in the saying, "an eye for an eye, and a tooth for a tooth"—an instinct which prompts and defends us in doing to another as he does to us, redeeming our pride from bondage to superior force. "Served him right" is the hearty response to an even retaliation.—The cordiality of this retaliation is founded mainly on the superior ability of the recipient to endure it, and react under it. The spleen, hardihood and strength of the aggressor graduate the rate of interest on the principal of injury he gives. When this hardihood gives way, and the beaten aggressor is a sufferer in his turn, then it becomes cruelty and persecution to beat him more. All giants and monsters are fair game:

they are to be freely tortured, until their extraordinary assurance falls—until the crisis of their mortal anguish bespeak the level of human sympathy. A fair fight, where either party stands up to his punishment, may be witnessed with some degree of pleasure; but a single blow given to a weak and retiring man rouses the wrath of all beholders; and he that strikes a fallen foe is dubbed a coward and a brute by all honorable men. When the courage and the fortitude are gone, or when remorse and repentance seize upon the soul of the criminal, the justice of nature is content.—But society has deemed it expedient to hang men, though the judge who sentences falters and chokes, and the hangman does his office with tears in his eyes,—while not a heart that beats in the presence of this sterner justice but wishes the criminal might escape unhurt. This is another kind of justice from that first spoken of—a justice founded on experience and observation—the justice of enlightened society. We have learned that it is not good to give blow for blow; we have also learned that men should be punished, although the men they grieved may afterward wish them at liberty. The social law takes no account of the peculiar resentment of the injured individual, and does not for the present punish either more or less therefor. It is as great a crime to strike a philosopher as to strike a fool. The law looks toward the injury of other men. The law punishes not for vengeance, but for protection; not for what men have done, but for what men may do hereafter. In the true spirit of social law, if henceforth there could be crime no more, but rather harmony and peace, all those offenders now incarcerated should go free at once. This is the justice of reason.

The justice of reason is the justice of policy. It is practical, rather than metaphysical. It takes no immediate cognizance of the origin of an evil nature, whether the will be of God or man; for its punishment is to the abatement of the nuisance, and looks no further. It punishes for the good of all men, the criminal included, if possible; but if he be deemed incorrigible, (which is a debatable presumption,) the law slays him without regard either to the origin of his vice or to his fate hereafter, whether death shall make him better or worse, happier or more miserable.—And as nations advance into enlightenment we find the justice of nature slowly fading out of the theory of law, vengeance giving place to reason, policy, and benevolence. As we rise in knowledge and self-respect, more and more clearly does crime appear social misfortune, more and more forgiving becomes human nature, in the belief that God rules the world, and more and more effort is encouraged to persuade the criminal that the law studies his interest as well as that of other men, and to make his punishment redound to his spiritual good.— In the light of this advancement, we may well prophesy the abolition of the death penalty. But its existence and its summary execution are in plain confirmation of this doctrine, that the justice of reason is the justice of expediency, independent of original desert,—although this expedient may not be in the best method for attaining the desired end.—The justice of nature is the justice of the mob, and the mother of lynch-law; but policy is the monitor of the cool and sapient judge, whose justice is founded on experience and reason.

Coeval with the adoption of the justice of reason and benevolence is the suspicion that God is not so weak that he need punish men either for his protection or his vengeance,—but that his inflictions are the growth of either love or hatred towards men.

And here we shall assert that the pain given of God to men has no absolute relation to the crimes and follies they have committed,—which crimes and follies we shall find to be but a diverting pretext, whereby the inferior man shall instinctively reproach himself rather than his Maker, whereby his good deeds and wise accomplishments may, through the same sense of independence from God, redound to his personal pride and exultation, while through this life and the lives to come God carries on the infinite system wherein both the crime and the penalty were equally just, expedient, and necessary for the greatest good of every living creature: and that while justice and expediency are one, the justice of men is born of fear and weakness, while God's justice is born of love and power.

We must distinguish between Right temporal, founded upon special law, and Right eternal, whereby law, the breach of law, and its penalty, as well as all other acts and things, are within the policy of the best eternal system. Crime, breaking the temporal law, is not right when judged thereby: and man under that law finds his duty still before him, and finds that the way of the transgressor is hard: though it needs be that offences come, yet wo unto the man by whom the offence cometh, temporally considered—more properly, in its immediate results. But eternal right, whereof is the righteousness of God, is above all law and punishment, of which it is the author, and is founded on eternal benevolence, working against eternal necessity, for the harmony of the universe. In the eye of this eternal right, the law and its violation are one, being equally good. Great is the law; but man is greater than all law, and dearer to the heart of the Almighty, who makes it apparently the temporal master, only that it may be in truth the eternal servant of the human race. The law was made to be broken, as well as to be kept, as an instrument for the advancement of man through experience. Perhaps no man ever lived a day without violating law; yet no violation of law can jar the harmony of the universe, for love is above all law. "The law was given that sin might abound; but where sin abounded, grace did even more abound."

We will delay here but a moment to remark—(for on so dry a matter we are fain to use all fair expedients so to sustain the curiosity of our reader that he may keep with us to the end, which shall explain all)—that the most flat and fruitless of all worlds imaginable were this world without those evils which men consider its especial curse. What has this whole race to do, but to supply its wants, and mitigate its evils ? How hard the ministers, doctors, editors, politicians, and the rest, are laboring for that "good of the race," which, if once accomplished, would throw them all out of employment, and leave them waiting for the heavens to come down. We want much: but to want these wants were worse than all.— And if any man say that nothing would please him better than idleness, he may have it. Down by the equator he shall want for neither food nor clothes, eating the bread-fruit and rolling on the sand. Who covets this felicity?

Section XII.

Social Relations

*I*t may occur to the reader that this is thus far a rude
and selfish philosophy. What! say you, is God as well
pleased that a man should lie, swear, steal, and do all un-
holy things, as that he should be virtuous, prayerful and
benevolent? Yea, verily—else is God of all beings the
most wretched, for blows and curses outnumber prayers
and alms. "Who is he that saith, and it cometh to pass,
and the Lord commanded it not?"—The exalted soul is
pleased at cursing and at blessing by times; and nothing
but his own interest and the interest of those in whom he
is concerned (who comprise the whole human race) shall
induce him to meddle in the matter.

When we set about to take care of ourselves, we find
that God has bound up our interest more or less with the
interests of all other men. It is apparently an idle speculation whether man is capable of disinterested benevolence,
for God has put it out of man's power to exercise it. We
cannot if we would sacrifice for the good of others without reaping a reward in the sense of our magnanimity,—
nor can we injure another without injury to ourselves
proportionate to our own estimate of the injury con-

ferred. Then why need we glorify ourselves with the conjecture that we should be equally benevolent though it were our eternal injury and discredit?

Let every man consult with perfect wisdom his individual interest, and the ends which society contemplates will be gained. The application of self-interest accounts for all man's social relations. If he suffers for his own ignorance and folly, so does he suffer for the defects of others, and these others for his; and his policy includes not only his own advancement but that of all with whom he is associated. Thus are we bound together. Benevolence—evangelization—all reformatory effort is our plain policy as a mass. For this we print books, found schools, hospitals, asylums, prisons, states, laws, all features of the body politic. Some of these bear the reputation of pure benevolence,—for all men do not see their policy, and some object to be taxed for them: yet they are politic, and the sure outgrowth of crescent civilization. And we shall not affirm but that time may remove some of these institutions by the light of the same policy in which they now exist.

Section XIII.

Classification Of Evils, And Some Deprecation Thereof

*W*hen the mind is relieved from any apprehension through "the exceeding sinfulness of sin," the evil of the world will resolve itself to pain and that which produces it; and good will resolve itself to joy and its efficients, all time being considered.—Before we can well understand how these evils are of use to us, and in harmony with the necessary nature of man, it will be necessary for us to separate and classify them, and observe briefly their secondary causes.

Firstly, there are evils of malice or depravity, evils we do ourselves and others, and evils which others do themselves and us; evils of violence, excess, and careless-ness, from which come also hereditary diseases, constitu-tional prostrations, fear, melancholy, and other personal discontents.

Secondly, there are evils of ignorance, from which come accidents, sundry fears and diseases, pestilence, witchcraft, superstition, together with straits and forced circumstances, out of which come misunderstandings, disputes, blows, calumnies, and strife.

Thirdly, there are evils called providences, as lightning, storm, earthquake, famine, and pestilence perhaps, with other occasions of sudden suffering and death.

Fourthly, there is the evil of labor by necessity, in order to health, spirit, and sustenance.

Death we shall omit from the present list, (for no man knows any evil of death but its fear,) and leave its qualities for future inference.

Before we seek any use, mitigation or compensation of our evils, we shall take leave to deprecate them.

How little is there of pain, compared with what the body may be fancied capable of suffering! How near we are to unconsciousness and death! The God of nature tunes our every string—he pumps the blood, he heaves the lungs, he keeps us altogether: and lo! with one little bone dislocated, we think God has deserted us!—with one little nerve in a tooth partially overflowed with blood, we think we smell hell fire, though all the rest of the system be working well. Yet all our teeth are capable of aching, and all our bones may be dislocated at once. God will not permit us to suffer so much; consciousness gives way,—we pass under the shadow of an angel's wing, and nature struggles for her liberty alone with God. Ah! to be God-forsaken—and reason still holding the throne of a soul whose body could not die—!—! if God meant to hurt us we should be hurt indeed.

And experience teaches us that there is a moral power in a well-wrought mind almost superior to all pain. The eye of the martyr, fixed on the throne of his divinity, will not see his quivering flesh. The heroes of Indian immolation,—the devotees who hang by hooks in their backs,—the wives who burn without a murmur on the pyres of their departed husbands, —the Montezuma smiling on his bed of roses,—what do these things tell us? There is God within us. Faith as a grain of mustard laughs at the pains we groan for. Not the body but the soul is the man. Rouse the soul and it cannot feel the body. Exalted, enraged, frightened, we may be hurt and know it not. Men have been mortally wounded, and scarcely knew it till their anger passed. Why, reader, as we muse on what we might be—as we look within and catch the eye of the genius that smiles us on,—as we think even of what some glorious hearts have suffered, beating in no better flesh than this of our's, we grow ashamed of these paltry metaphysics,—we could dash pen and paper on the ground, and scorn ourself that we ever sought God's purpose in pains and sorrows which so many brave have smiled to encounter.

From this lofty self-possession we turn with contempt to the converse abnegation wherein lies all the fear and folly of the world. "Know ye not, brethren, that to whom ye yield yourselves servants to obey, his servants ye are?" The witch-believer will be bewitched; the Methodist will be thrown by the Power; the Dervish will dance, and the Medium will turn bloodless, as the spirits they yield to clutch at their consent. But the royal soul may be above the charms of the charmer, and dictate the coming of its angels and its fiends.

It is a good thing to think of, that we are better prepared to judge our troubles when they have passed than
while their stress is on us. If a man is in an ill humor,
and knows that its cause was some certain irregularity,
he knows how long it should last; and this knowledge,
timely thought of, will diminish that pain by half. If
our troubles slay us, there needs proof that we shall not
immediately rejoice therefor; and if we survive them,
there are always considerations which make us not sorry
to have suffered. Who so proud as he that has suffered?
The least complaint of another provokes his self-conceit.
No soldier was ever ashamed of his scars. No athlete was
ever sorry for the care and exertion which his high condition cost him. And so the exercise of pain and care
and sorrow, which develop the intellectual gladiator and
make him strong by experience and insight, is never remembered but with pride and pleasure. A thousand years
of suffering are but as yesterday when it is past: but the
present pride of a lofty soul sends light and glory over all
the future.

Another good thought in regard to all pain is that the
silent forces of nature hate it, and react against it. Much
of the healing art consists in removing the hindrances to
nature's generous wish, to heal, to get well, and to grow.
In nature lies all skill and safety. Find out her methods,
and we shall seldom go amiss. How often we hear courses recommended as the most natural,—as though nature
were wholly reliable.

It will be well for us also to observe how many of

these evils are within the voluntary power of the race, —or what portion of them the race may blame itself for.

All hereditary evils are of course unavoidable as such by posterity; but if they came of human volition primarily, they may be classed as in one sense avoidable. And these may, for the most part, be mitigated by us, and if not eradicated, at least sent to the next posterity with less virulence than they came to this.

All the evils of malice come from the human will, and these it is but for the race itself to say it will avoid. And for those brutal and imbecile beings so low that men have accounted them irresponsible, we know very well what causes tend to their production. Excess, violence, intermarriage, uncleanness, all help to beget a fool or a madman. The vices we encourage in ourselves not only corrupt our blood and breed, but they weaken those virtuous instincts in our posterity on which alone can be predicated the improvement of after times. A man may vitiate his posterity beyond their power of recuperation; but he cannot make them infallibly virtuous. Hence "the evil that men do lives after them—the good is oft interred with their bones."

The evils of ignorance may be spoken of as evils of necessary and of unnecessary ignorance. These evils altogether bear no comparison with the evils of malice. Did we but use with unfailing virtue the knowledge we have, there would be few complaints of evils necessary. We know well enough, and early enough, that temperance and exercise are necessary to good health: heeding what we know, we might have sound minds in sound bodies, comparatively speaking, in defiance of what we know not,—and having these, we should defy fear and melancholy, and many other personal discontents. Doubtless there are evils growing of necessary ignorance: man has not mastered the ways of nature, and many events now deemed unavoidable may yet subserve the skill of science. Lightning, of all things, was as the hand of God to the ancients. "Canst thou send the lightning?" Yea, we can. And who shall declare it improbable that man shall yet control the pressure of the winds, bring rain from the clouds, and soothe the breast of the sea? Then pestilence and famine may become creatures of human wilfulness and neglect. Though there be calamities which no foresight nor prudence may intercept,—though the most cautious foot will slip, and the best judgment be at fault,—though our faculties be imperfect and our attention abstracted,—though the earth has pitfalls, and reptiles and wild beasts of sudden presence,—though a thousand things are straining which lack but the last hair to break them, and a thousand arts hang just within a wink of discovery, yet while that which we do know is not regarded in our own behalf, it is with an ill grace that we complain of the tyranny of that which we know not—of evils which we cannot control—which, though controllable, were as readily neglected as those now under command.

Section XIV.

The Finite Cannot Be Perfectly Happy

This brings us to where we shall boldly declare that none of these aches and fears and discontents are of themselves evils in the world; but they comprise the lower half of a necessary and beautiful variety, better than any supposable monotony without them. The only evil is the necessity that, if we exist at all, we must be less than God—an evil without the scope of omnipotence or benevolence, and a misfortune attributable to divine malice only when men shall prefer nonentity to life. If any man did ever so prefer we know it not; but we know that to most men the thought were madness. The ancient wished that he never had been born; yet he lived to glorify God's providence. The point is beyond controversy, save by inference; and we pass on to find benevolence in the method of our existence, rather than in the fact.

It is not generally the pain, the labor, the care, and fear, in themselves, which trouble man and make him speculate: he has seen some good, some compensation for each one of these: evil is not a practical, so much as a theoretical problem. We cry out, "If God can make us happy, why cannot he leave us so?—all this ingenious utility, variety, beauty, mitigation, and compensation—they amount to no prime and satisfying reason why there should be any pain or discontent whatsoever."—We answer, Though God be the perfection of all benevolence and power, he cannot make man continually happy. The God within us knows the God without us, and the pent essence struggles for the level of its source. Our ideals despise us: nor can we go so high but we can see something higher. We shall not complain of God; but God in us shall complain—complain at confinement, complain at imperfection, complain at our finitude in general, which yet it shall know to be necessary to what happiness we do obtain. We must be finite: and now, how shall the finite be made happy? We answer, only by just such an existence as this of ours is and promises to be, can man obtain the greatest happiness of which God's creatures are capable.—If this does not sound very encouraging, let us remark that it is not so bad a state of things as might be at first supposed. Though we should say, We have been as happy as we ever shall be—as happy on the road to "heaven" as we shall ever be when we "get there,"—though we should say that we have been as happy as eternal progress will ever make us, still we have our heaven—a higher, brighter, prouder heaven than Zealot ever sung in praise of.

What is this happiness, its abode and genealogy?

The first lesson in human philosophy—the common-

est wit in the world is this: What will make us happy cannot keep us so. And the second is like unto it: Happiness
does not consist in things external, nor things internal,
but in the correlation of the mind to the world. Neither
appetite nor victual alone can make a feast; but as these
two come together, each destroying the other, happiness is the result of the proceeding. After the feast the
memory for a while sustains the happiness. And in due
time the anticipation of another feast brings further joy.
Ambition has bred more joy than the goals it sought for.
We grow gradually rich, and we think we should thereby grow gradually happier, attaining that on which our
joy seems to depend. But it proves otherwise: for rich,
from the rich man, is generally as far as from the poor.
Beginning life, we would be content with ten thousand:
we gain this, and riches are still ahead; reaching a hundred thousand, if we formally pause there, we soon find
it as hard to keep our wealth as if we were gaining more;
at best we are no happier than at first. The first dollar
earned, like the first love of the heart, is a joy that comes
but once. What we gain in pride over our wealth we lose
in the carelessness of poverty, or the excitement of eager
ambition. But if, with a philosophical spirit, we sought a
hundred thousand, gained it, and have enough, then it is
not long till we learn that money is not what we want.
We would give half our wealth for some one's health,
strength, beauty, wit, spirit, fame—something which
heretofore we did not care or wish for. And if we have
all—wit and fame, knowledge and influence, spirit and

81

standing, health and hope, tact and success, we shall not live long. Nature cannot support such prodigality; and in a quarrel, or with some disease, she cuts the darling off.

Now why is this—the thing that pleases us to-day, and makes us happy, has not the power to do it tomorrow? There is but one reason: we have outgrown it. The soul has expanded, and that thing cannot fill it. The soul is the great critic: it can appreciate better things than it can produce: it stands on its dignity, and refuses to be pleased. What is our Shakspeare to the Shakspeare of Shakspeare? Yet what were he to the ever-expanding soul, whose thought there has been neither patience, wit, nor courage to write down? All things present themselves to the soul with averted eyes; they are but the regrets and compliments of the great truth that is unavoidably detained; and the soul accepts them as apologies from the infinite Perfect which alone could satisfy it. Present any thing,—the soul will outgrow it. There is an infinite maw, of which what we are wont to call ourselves is but the mouthpiece, which can swallow all the future, and comprehend, contain, outgrow the whole universe of God. This maw must be fed, and that with fresh food. If we shall live forever we must swallow all things and digest them; little by little we must eat up sun, moon and stars. We must have eternal news from God. Our souls are strung upon knowledge like beads: it passes through us, it polishes us, and ceases to be of absorbing interest. Once the picture of a battle pleased us: now the battle itself grows dull. We forget our baby consciousness, and live but where we are. Our life is as the deep, its bottom towards the centre; and we live only in the upper surface—the foam that grows by the agitation of the wind. We cannot be satisfied; we cannot be filled. More! More! shouts the soul. She shakes her chain, and the hills of the earth and the fixed stars of heaven echo and re-echo her cry, "Excelsior! Excelsior!" Reason would teach us that this divine captive must advance if she would not be wretched; and experience confirms the judgment, and sounds through all her avenues the broad Amen.

We have heard good fellows, warm with wine, wish they might live forever as they were. They did not know themselves. Place man in Paradise, perfect in all things but knowledge and power, and he will not remain: he will experiment—he will do some thing for better or for worse. Reader, perhaps you have been sick,—you have languished for the green fields and the pleasant sun. At length, after weary weeks, came convalescence; you went out into the clear air, and all was beautiful. The sun shone on the waving grass as he never shone before; the bluebird warbled a celestial music; a thousand swallows cut the heavens with wings of steel; and high imagination looked beyond the distant peaks, and spotted the round world with nations; you gave yourself up utterly to the hour, without hope or thought beyond—more than warm, intoxicated with the wine of new life:—yet before the sun went down your soul had almost outgrown its beautiful new world,—you were almost as indifferent as before sad illness had arrested your career.

"Ah!—but if I could *remain* thus happy!—I know that I weary; but let me remain thus happy, and I should be content."—Aye, this were joy indeed. But see you not that for you to remain thus happy the world must ever increase its beauty?—Will you accept the knowledge of good and evil—the secrets of the gods—the Promethean spark? Will you be half divine, and know that there is an infinite Perfect beyond you? Then God cannot make you such that the same things shall satisfy you forever. Nature and truth cannot improve; therefore you, who live on truth and beauty, must have more and more forever.

Then you will say, "If there is any wish in heaven that I should be happy, and if happiness lies in progression, why cannot I begin lowly, and constantly progress, without these torturing changes into woe,—every new day being higher, brighter, wiser, freer than the last?" We answer, you are reaching your own wish, by the wisest, in short, the only method; yet never can be continually happy.

When we examine our lives and consciousness, we become aware of an equator in our experience, whose name is Law, above which lies our joy, and below which lies our pain. Each man lives his own life, and no other: his highest joy is the highest joy he knows; his lowest grief is the lowest he has conceived; and between these is an average line, or an equator of consciousness, self-established, which is the tenor of his life. The time occupied will not matter; he may have grown old in an hour, or the memory of an hour's joy may have lighted years of weariness,—still his life will have its equator; and he never can know whether another man's life was happier than his own.

Though crippled or sickened from infancy or youth,—though broken or ruined in manhood, let no man judge him, for God is with him as with Crœsus and Apollo. He has his good times. His life is his own; he knows no other, nor of any other can he judge. Not health, nor wealth, nor beauty, nor troops of friends, nor peals of laughter, can ever prove that Alexander on his Bucephalus was happier than Diogenes in his tub.

Granting your request, that man's life should be one even, monotonous ascent, even though it were from what we now call happy to happier, we must still find, in all that each man has lived of life, this same equator, this average consciousness, known by memory of the past: for although now the equator bear the name of Law, above which we have found our joy, and below which we have found our woe, still will it exist, by the necessity of finite life, which, coming short of perfection, can only be more or less imperfect. Examine yourself, and you will find that you consider yourself more or less happy according to what you have experienced heretofore. Therefore we have no reason to suppose that a higher beginning and a higher grade of life would in any manner change the necessities which are over us; and the present life, from the height of its joy to the depth of its woe, in the course of thirty years, is as capable of illustrating your notion of progression as would be a life which began where this one should leave off, and be continued thirty years thereafter.

Taking the present life then for an illustration: Would it be better that man should have such an even rate of progression that a superior intelligence could calculate his equator by knowing the number of his days;—or that each new day should reveal to him events from various portions of his entire grade which put its equator beyond finite suspicion:—in other words, would it be better for man to begin life at his lowest misery, even at the last gasp of mortal agony, and slowly and evenly progress until he should reach a whole week of hearty laughter, or a week of heartfelt joy, at the age of 30 years; or to begin life as he now does, with living instead of dying sensations, growing through a careless youth to the cares, toils, fortunes and misfortunes of manhood, mingling his joys and sorrows, now a touch of ecstacy and now a twinge of the heart-ache, without any other consciousness of ascent than that of ever-increasing wisdom?—This gives us startling thought. What! Shall we begin in misery, and never smile for fifteen years?—nay, twenty-five? We find, thankfully, that the average plane of our lives would be far lower than we had anticipated. There are but five or six days of laughter—scarce a month of contentment in a whole lifetime. And when we further reflect that in either case the future, even as now, must be as now unknown,—for the knowledge of the future must be as now, an infinite knowledge, to share which were to dethrone the Almighty in universal confusion,—the scheme becomes altogether unpromising.

Give us a joy in our youth, and that joy draws interest for years. The memory of it is joy; the hope of its recurrence is joy, for it points to the probability of joy hereafter; and this hope is a stay to our existence. But how can we be said fairly to anticipate, or eagerly to hope for a joy which we have never conceived, or felt in our experience? This joy, though it may prove the highest joy of our grade, is worth more in the middle of our life than at the end, because of its encouragement. But our pains, at the same time, draw little interest of their kind: on the contrary, they are a source of pride; they leave no sting behind, but rather knowledge and caution, which diminish pain in perspective; and they are stimuli and warning, without which our bodies would not endure a year.—Above all, the life is full of novelty for the ever-wakeful curiosity of the soul. "Who knoweth what a day may bring forth?"—Here is economy—the most is made of a certain amount of joy, and the least is made of any given amount of pain. But where no ray of hope from a blessing in the past pointed with cheer to the happiness of the future, we should moan at every trivial advance, "and is this all?"—But why *all*? From what could we prophesy that there was better to be expected? Nay, instead of holding to a belief that we were advancing, we should be certain that each day increased our wretchedness,—our grade would point downward, and we should never smile—never, while the heavens beheld us.

It is in the nature of the immortal finite to hate monotony. We know there exists perfection, and we desire to taste it. Aught that recurs loses its interest, and its hold on our attention. The clock strikes seventy-eight times in twelve hours, and after half of those hours, no one in the house can tell you whether the clock has struck at all! What is half an inch of advance per day to the growing soul? We prefer our joys intense, though our pains be intense also. Men will be drunk a week, though they should be sick a fortnight. These excesses remind man of his possible destiny, and, as promises, are beneficial to the soul; and their benefit to the soul reacts upon the body which at first suffers by them. Corpulation is a bodily excess; the body is immediately weakened thereby; and perhaps no brute is at any time the better for it. But man is. Perfect continence is good for a time; yet in a few months the mind is injured thereby; the spirits lose elasticity; a source of joy, anticipation, and memory is cut off; and the body suffers in the want of this exercise of the mind, unless the mind be philosophically fortified. For these reasons, based upon practical life, we must conclude that if life is to advance at all, (which we have not presumed) we shall prefer that our joys and sorrows be scattered over each life, without regard to rotation in their degrees of intensity. We shall prefer a foretaste of the future, by way of assurance, stimulus, and consolation. We would not wish to feel that we are climbing toward the infinite one round at a time. Rather would we scan this life while each new day should vary our weird path, and bring us we know not what or where,—and then let the Power suddenly take us by the hand and jerk us through the blue universe a myriad leagues at once, till the status of every advance shall charm us as the resurrection of the dead. We may be affrighted—we will be affrighted,—we may suffer—we will suffer,—but O! thou infinite Perfection, bid us not hourly remember that the Tower of Baal was no nearer to heaven than the rock it stood on!

You will not confuse this matter with sophistry, as thus: "New truth and beauty make men happy,—and as the universe is infinite, there is no reason that should prevent the continual passage of beauty and truth before him,—thus making him continually happy, by keeping up with the expansion of the soul."—Upon what do you predicate the soul's capacity to expand, or deny that new truth is constantly presented? Have you found that novelty, either in sight or speed, which will not cease to charm you? Then you have found the philosopher's stone, perpetual motion, and the fountain of youth. The soul would hate a regular expansion. It would be God in a moment, if it could. Say to yourself, *happy, happy, happy,* a hundred times, and the word will mean nothing. Happiness is nothing absolute; penny happy or pound happy is the same. The child with his new toy, or the king with his new crown, or God with all the universe can but be happy; the soul can but be filled; and the consciousness of fulness can be predicated, (save in the consciousness of *infinite* fulness,) only on the memory of emptiness; and to *be* happy, happy, happy, is as useless to the soul as to *say* it. Say that truth and beauty produce happiness: what is truth? *Truth is every thing:* truth is as much in pain as it is in pleasure. It is as much in slow expansion as in swift expansion. We must be wretched for truth's sake. What is beauty? it is harmony and law relieved against chaos and deformity. Nothing can you possess, (baring that you possess it to *immediate infinity,*) that can keep the soul full. The fault is not in our grade, but in our nature. Adam and Eve outgrew the walls of Eden—how soon! The highest harp in heaven jars with the same discord, of the same amount in proportion to its grade. The giant is at Gabriel's elbow as he is at yours: his grade is higher, but is still a grade, and had it been his first grade, he were as uneasy in it as you are in yours.— The point we start from matters nothing, and neither does the speed; so neither does the steepness of the ascent. You may object, "That it is because the plane of our life here would ascend as it were too few inches to the foot, that we should cease to feel the ascent. But set it perpendicular, and give us lightning speed; let us feel in an hour the joys of youth, the first dawn of love, the excitements of passion and ambition, and the triumph over death: let the Almighty tax his strength to lift us, and we should be happy." This is an error in logic, and a presumption in defiance of experience. Doubtless in memory of your past experience, now, such a rate would please you for a time; but it were only because of your past experience,—and time would as surely balance you into a monotony of consciousness as hopeless and barren as that we first supposed, as it would in a grade whose speed and ascent were but as from our lowest misery to our highest joy in thirty years.

See you not an object in the slowness of our ascent? It is that we may learn *all*, truly, surely, and well,—learn that the universe is full. Such is the expansive force of the soul that, two truths being presented, a greater and a lesser, the lesser will be slighted for the greater. Give us a series of truths,—the soul will seize first that which is greatest. Give the soul its choice, and its first demand is, what is the prime secret and power of the universe? And of any series of truths, it first seizes those salient features which best tend to answer this question,—while the minor truths are learned only by force of leisure;—yet each of these is as capable of pleasing the soul as the greater truths, when that soul is so diverted by the flesh that was made to confine it that the thought of infinity is abstracted therefrom.—Go to the great galleries where the genius of a thousand years is hung against the walls, and begin to examine. While you gaze at the first picture, a glimpse of the second distracts your attention, and you pass to that; from this the third attracts you,—and from this the fourth is calling: soon you are in motion: you wander on, for novelty,—past works that have cost toil and skill, and are full of beauty,—but you are in motion,—you want novelty, novelty: like an ox in a fresh field, you cannot stop to eat until you have been all around it,—you would know if there is a picture there as good as you can appreciate—one that shall strike you dumb. But you do not find it. Wearied and disgusted that the gallery is not of infinite extent, that you might walk on, run, fly, for first impressions only, till you find the Perfect picture, you who came to spend the whole day go home e'er it is noon. Morning dawns,—the flesh is rested,—the bedeviled curiosity of the infinite is quiet, —and lo! the little picture over the mantel attracts you for an hour: how softly the shadows fall! how plain the dark and straggling foliage stands against the sky! how well the ripples break the reflections in the lake!—Why, here is more pleasure than the whole gallery of yesterday afforded!—Do you see why this is?—It is because the whole gallery was as one picture, or one curiosity, and you did not stay to comprehend it: your progress roused the infinite passion, and turned what was a line of beauties into a line of novelties. When you have compassed the exhibition,—assured yourself of the truth that there is nothing there to content you, or astonish you, then you may haunt the gallery for days and days, and feast upon the beauties which the love and hope of the great Perfect drove entirely out of sight on your first perusal.—And who are these minor beauties meant for, if not for you? True, the universe is an infinite gallery; it also is true that we shall traverse it in infinite time; but of what use were it to squander its beauty, gaining no joy thereby, but only increasing our curiosity, which we know cannot be satisfied? And these minor truths were once the height of your comprehension. Besides, we shall see anon a utility and beauty, (which just here we are not altogether ready to appreciate,) in the existence of infinitely various grades of intelligences, which shall peruse at the same time various grades of truth and beauty,—in which variety of intelligences there must be somewhere such beings as man and boy. The universe is full: and would you destroy all that amused your youth, because you are a man?

The sum of this discussion is, that pain is necessary to all finite pleasure. The soul cannot be placed where it will not expand, and pine for alternation. It chafes against its finite bonds, which being enlarged a little, it feels free for a moment, and instantly grows up to them, to be chafed again. All that we get is good, but it is good, as food is, only for once eating; time and the expansion of the soul turn it to evil, compared with what it was.—What we urge is that inasmuch as we cannot have perfect freedom, it is better that we have our progression in a varied rather than a monotonous manner,—better to have pain and pleasure in some intensity than to have a lukewarm sensation between them,—better that we chafe in our bonds, and then have sudden liberty, than that in an even and regular manner we should insensibly expand, —better by this much: that the soul has a pleasure in change, even though it did not progress,—while it has pain in monotony, even though progressive.

God has placed all things at an infinite distance from his perfection, that he may make them happy by drawing them forever towards it. We retain the love of our existence in the consciousness of this transition state. Only that which is down can ever get up; only rising can keep the soul from wretchedness,—and it cannot rise to light without having darkness to rise from. Hunger is the seasoning of the feast; and pain is the foundation of all finite pleasure, as the lower stone supports the upper.

> "Eterne alteration
>   Now follows, now flies:
> And under pain pleasure,
>   Under pleasure pain lies."

Section XV.

Each For All

 $\mathcal{J}$ f then, up to this time, we have learned that the imperfection and confinement of the human soul are necessary to the harmonious government of the universe;
and that expansion is necessary to any finite happiness,
in any grade of our existence,—we are now prepared to
say that we shall be contented with God's method in us,
providing we shall hereafter find that this finitude is so
operated as to give us the greatest amount of pleasure and
progress of which we shall conclude this first grade of
man capable. Some pain being necessary, do we receive
it in the best time and method.

When we undertake to pass upon the propriety of
God's dealings with us, we must still bear in mind a
former position: that each of us, as finite beings, cannot
comprise any perfect system as individuals; we are but
imperfect parts of one entire perfect system. If, therefore,
an individual find himself wanting in any special merit,
or sacrificing any special good, he will attribute the fact
to the necessity of finite imperfection; at the same time
he may be grateful, if what he lacks is by that lack made
the peculiar comfort of another man, and if what he sac-

rifices does some other being good;—for hereby he may discover that nothing is absolutely evil, nor made nor done in vain, but that some other man's evil is his peculiar good. He will observe how, in business, the wants of one man bring joy and fortune to another. Does he long for a picture? The artist is glad. Does he need a physician? The doctor is glad. Does the doctor lose his case? The undertaker is glad; and so on. One man's meat is another man's poison.

> "Fleas have other fleas to bite 'em—
>   And so go on, ad fin*i*tum."

If for any wise purpose of variety or harmony life varies from the infinite to the infinitessimal, there must be somewhere such a thing as man: and if for the same reason the human race varies from Shakspeare and Bacon to an idiot, there must be somewhere such a man as you are. All cannot be the head, but some must be the hands, and legs, and baser parts. None can be made for itself alone, but each for all,—for the edification and amusement of the entire race. One must furnish beauty, and lose something thereby; another must furnish deformity, and have some compensation therefor. One must furnish black eyes, another blue. One must furnish faculty, another capacity. One must be an example of suffering, and another must die of joy. Each man's actions must refer to the actions of all other men. You are born, like Caligula, or Socrates, to be a specimen, a curiosity, or perhaps a by-word,—"to make little boys ask questions." The sufferings of Job were not for Job alone, else we never should have heard of Job. The rare breed of fish that was hauled from the deep to-day lived since the beginning of its species unknown of men till now, partly that we might wonder why it was hid from us so long. There have been rainbows, gems, and shells, and birds of heavenly plumage that perished unseen of men, away in the forgotten youth of the Almighty; dark plagues have wrapped in frightful death their millions unrecorded, and the cries of famished nations have pierced the dome of heaven, partly to excite our restless souls, and make us wonder at the ways of God. So when we suffer, we are making food for the soul of man: and if no eye beholds our suffering save the eye of our Father in heaven, we do not suffer in vain, either for ourselves or others. Have not we been fed with the thought that many a poor fellow has poured out his soul to God in the wilderness, or on a wreck, or shut in the horrid bowels of the earth, where none but the Almighty listened? Did not He teach us that these things are true, we should not believe them. We cannot have fiction without truth, nor dreams without experience. All things are inspired by one Being, to one end. There is no imposture, waste, nor confusion, but an infinite variety, fitted to the infinite destiny of the soul. And many a calamity, dark and terrible, has cut men off from this world (perchance into a better) that we might wonder rather than despair.

The only limit that benevolence will prescribe to this

variety is, that its extremities should not proceed so far as to produce unmitigated and uncompensated evil. If Samson was the strongest of men, or if Goliath of Gath was the largest of men, we shall require that these were strong and large enough; and that for them to have been stronger, or larger, were to have produced absolute evil. And truly, a man who could slay a thousand Philistines with the jaw of an ass is a sufficient specimen of strength: while a man who could handle a spear like a weaver's beam cannot be improved, though Milton give the devil a spear as big as the mast of a ship.—And so of the varieties of nature. If we shall suppose man fitted to the earth, then although the earth should pass through the greatest variety of changes, the same general features should be renewed. We cannot expect that nature should be so fitful as to stand on her head for one generation's amusement, while other beings are hourly born, for whose similar natures she is meant to smile and frown as well as for us.

Above all things the finite soul demands that such a variety should exist: for novelty, or change, and progression are one. Moreover we shall demand that this variety be so distributed that all shall find something pleasing in it, rather than that some should be nearly perfect, and others utterly neglected. We would ask that he who bears the burden of painful experience should have some compensation therefor, and strength to his task. And further, inasmuch as it is the exaltation of our intellects which has led us into the comparison of finite and infinite, by which comparison we suffer, shall we not ask that as much of the old stupidity—the brute consciousness of the unspeculative period be granted to us as the progress of our grade will permit of? And lastly, if there should appear to be suffering for which our judgments do not find entire compensation in this life, we shall ask that it be of such a character that the style which reason gives to the next grade of our immortal life shall be such as to fill the compensation of that peculiar suffering more especially. We say this at a peradventure. Personally we have known no past calamity for which we are not compensated, or for which we do not see clear promises of compensation here. But some may think otherwise. And to such we say, If the vast majority of your ills are compensated, cannot you take the remainder upon trust, and use it as a proof that you will live again, that the balance may be fully settled which is here so plainly begun and proceeding? We say this because some men who may read this have not the skill in human motives and intellectual influences to determine what a compensation is,—and not because we recede from our proposition that there is no absolute or God-sanctioned evil on earth. Even if there were evils for which no other man sees compensation on earth, we have pointed at that compensation— the hope which the unbalanced account should afford of a life hereafter, where that which here began may find accomplishment.

Try the world by these demands—call thou, and let her answer.

Section XVI.

Variety

*T*here is a proverb among men that no two things are exactly alike; "You cannot bathe twice in the same river," said the ancient; but in the course of ordinary thought we do not reflect upon the truth and beauty of the saying. Let us dwell upon it, for it is blessed.—Turn not to the stars of differing glory, symbols of the human race, and ranging from the golden sun through a myriad galaxies whose snowing numbers drift into the Milky Way, but turn to our own star, Earth. Say first, thou sceptic of divine benevolence, why, in that revolution which brings light for all labor, and darkness for all rest,—why does she not turn plumb upon her axis, like all the wheels that man has put in motion? What dull mechanic boxed her widely-oscillating journals?— Glorious ecliptic! beauty of the material universe! thy designer is the friend of man: Winding, in the "line of beauty," the green and white around the varied world, bringing bright summer and gray winter to him who could love neither one alone. Would he have all cold, he can have it. Would he have all hot, he can have it. Would he stand still, and have every grade of hot and cold that his nature can endure, he can have them in one year's passage. Is a year too long—the steamers that round Cape Horn can put him almost a year into a month: Or let him climb a tropical mountain to its icy scalp, and encounter all the zones of the world. Loves he the short day or the long—he may choose. Would he try days without nights, or nights without days—he may prefer, and be gratified.—And every day is a little year on its own account—a wheel within a wheel. From darkness and repose pours up the gray light of the morning, through a pageant of clouds designed for this day only, and amid the hum of living nature the flowers open their dewy eyes. Slowly the day-summer rises to its tropical noon, and slowly it goes down into the artic-darkness, beyond the western waves. Then darkness deepens, and lo! the auroral stars, that wax and wane through the cold, delicious umbrage of the night, while, hour by hour, new constellations glad the feasting eye with their olden silver service—an heir-loom of the world.—And man, who beholds all this, and partly for whose pleasure all these were created, has his ecliptic also, and his wheel within a wheel. Through the windings of recorded civilization— through the golden ages that harden into the iron and the brass, and then refine to gold again,—through the dark ages and the bright, through reigns of terror and reigns of Saturn, through reigns of philosophy and reigns of madness, man has not been twice alike from the hour of his birth. We are older every moment; we have new accessions of experience, new styles of consciousness, and we see things in a different light. "All the world's a stage"—a stage with new proscenium and decorations nightly, and a change of play: there is many a spicy, quarrelsome recast, and an audience and actors whom we never saw before.

Section XVII.

Compensation

$\mathcal{W}$e must agree with those loving philosophers who hold it incorrect to impugn the providence of God for any circumstance which apparently finds compensation neither in this world nor the next; for there is a possibility of the imperfection of our vision; and there is many a good providence in our memory which requires the wisdom of centuries to heartily approve it. But when we come to look for an event which (judged by those laws of mind which experience has taught us) does no being good, or is not for the general good of all being, we shall be troubled to find one. It is indeed an ill wind that blows nobody good. There is a balance or compensation in nature, founded partly on those necessities of finite consciousness which we have exhibited, which cannot be disturbed. As in the sea, when a wave rise, a hollow must be left, so in the moral world, and in individual experience, there is a horizontal line, all prominence above which leaves a counterpart hollow below. This horizontal line is the equator of the moral world and universe. And as agitation is to the beauty and purity of the sea, so is it to the diversion and progression of man.

In the distribution of the world's variety, by the necessity of this balance, every peculiar experience, pleasant or painful—above or below the equator of consciousness—has a peculiar counterpart, whereby every pride must be humbled, and every envy comforted in the sight of foreign misfortune. This is the office of that "great Nemesis, who never yet of human wrong left the unbalanced scale." If one end of the beam is up, the other will be down. If one end of the needle is positive, the other must be negative. How else can one be positive than while the other is negative? If one end of a piece of mechanism has motion, the opposite end has power: you cannot add to the motion without adding to the power; nor the converse. You cannot make perpetual motion for want of perpetual power: yet there is perpetual motion, and the secret of it lies in the only safe of the universe— the infinite force of God. So is perpetual happiness a secret in the same keeping; and the same balance that exists in the principles of power and motion, or of positive, and negative in electricity, or in the variation of the waves from the proper perimeter of the globe, exists in the pain and pleasure of the soul, and in the whole moral world. We do not ask this of experience or observation; it is a deduction from the great premise of our treatise, the necessity of one God.

Yet turn to experience, and according to the force and subtilty of the intellect applied, you will see the compensation of all calamity, and the evil of all good that is good only by law.

Compensation

There is a saying of Edmund Burke, that no man had ever a point of pride that did not injure him, nor a defect that did not serve him. The crippled leg makes the cautious traveller, and spares the head many a bruise. There was once a stag that was proud of his horns, and ashamed of his legs. But the hounds of the hunter came upon his reverie, and the despised legs bore him away in safety until his proud horns caught fast in a thicket,— and he was slain. It frequently happens that the souls of men outgrow the love of their own peculiar merits, and they long to exchange, even for merits of less worth.— "There is a crack in every thing that God has made;" but through that crevice enters the light of heaven. Every thing is blessed, but every thing is unfortunate as well. If we run to brain, we will diminish in muscle: if we run to invention, we will diminish in execution. He that can invent has not the faculty to sell an invention: the ready, versatile tactician seldom can invent. If we conquer evils with science, we lose the victory in the carelessness of pride. Possession increases the appetite for possession, or else satiates to a want of the wants which that possession can gratify. He that is hungry, with nothing to eat, can see plenty of men who would do as much for his appetite as he would do for their provision. He that is injured by over-working shall see plenty dying of idleness; and he that is dying of starvation may see plenty dying of gluttony. It is all one to be smothered, whether with kisses or with ditch-water. He that has no special misfortune to trouble him may see the man of troubles grow strong in soul, while the listless shall stagnate in inertness. He shall find the man of labor full of health and spirit. He shall find that if the hard tool blisters the tender hand, the hand will grow fit for its mission, and will wax instead of waning. And he that has hands fit for the sledge cannot make watches nor drill needles. He that is a poet, sensitive and impressible, cannot be competent to the sudden strategem and dangerous reckoning of the field of battle. He that is impressible must be impressed,—he must both suffer and enjoy with more intensity than he that is full of the sturdy confidence of vigorous life.

This compensation shows itself in all business, and makes the proverbs of society. There is a sure watch on all benefits, that no man shall take a good thing without an evil thing. Every thing has a twin brother, an equivalent, a price. Nothing can be stolen: *cash* is the word, and no trust. Would you buy health?—labor and temperance are the price. Will you have a spree?—blues, nervousness, and moroseness. And these prices are low. It is easier to earn money than to steal and conceal it. Few men ever get rich by stealing or by gambling; or if they do, gold depreciates in their hands. The cost makes the value, in the estimate of the soul. Working men try to save their money; but inherited or stolen fortunes are considered scarcely worth saving. There is no good without sacrifice to pay for it. You can get only your money's worth in the end. Hire a boy to do a man's business; he will make up his wages in the spoiling of your tools. Though he may do well for a while, some accident will revenge your penuriousness. Is stolen fruit the sweetest? It needs to be, for the way of the transgressor is hard. Can the tough head bear the hard blows? It well may, for it is sure to get them. The solid tooth comes out hard. And the more life there is in us the harder we die. The animal compensates the spiritual, and the spiritual compensates the animal. Bodily pleasures detract from the spiritual fortune. Sensuality, intemperance, the use of tobacco and opium, all have a spiritual price. Anodynes, cathartics, diuretics, all have accounts with each other. And the nobler virtues and attainments cost also. Learning costs labor; memory costs experience; fortitude costs trial and suffering; charity costs money; and proven courage costs danger and the risk that so often ends in wooden legs, and medals that had as well been leather.

We mark this compensation in nature, and somewhat among brutes. The severity of the climate brings forth in time the fur necessary to make it comfortable: even torrid animals, taken to frigid zones, become so pilous in time as to endure the climate. All animals not otherwise protected grow hairy in winter. The horse too poor to own a blanket soon shivers himself into the favor of nature, and he gets a blanket that will not blow off until spring. Thus there is a compensation between heat, or fat, and hair. There are many nostrums for making hair grow: these are the best ones: cold and indigestion.— The storm is terrible; but the storm is only the other end of that sultry heat which is necessary to the creamy pulp of every pleasant fruit. And as storms cure the air, diseases cure the body of man. Disease is the balancing of the books of bodily life. Suppose there should come no compensation afterwards; perchance the compensation went before; but there is compensation afterwards as well.

Everywhere we turn our eyes but to behold some manner of compensation. We have taken great pleasure in a volume of criminal history now in our possession. How certain is the retribution of crime! He that has the disposition for evil never has the wit for concealment. Murder will out. The brand of Cain is on it. Look where men of known sagacity have committed murder: they became fools incontinently. Men who in their cooler moments could devise a hundred ways to murder without a chance of detection, when once the love of blood enters their hearts become incapable of deception.

Still, as we go on, a compensation for the stings of conscience and the sense of degradation shows itself in men's lives. The idle, the vagrant and the vicious—the loafer, the robber, the drunkard, the prostitute, all grow in an exaltation of the moral or enduring nature—in a sense of lofty though occasional liberty, which none better than the outcast can understand. There is a charm in the consciousness of vagrancy—a spirit that cries out

> "A fig for those by law protected!
>   Liberty's a glorious feast;
> Courts for cowards were erected—
>   Churches built to please the priest!"

Compensation

There is pride and power in the defiance of law; —
"and the joy that is sweetest lurks in stings of remorse."—
Of all men, the sailor, in his sea-girt prison, leads a life
most monotonous: yet is he a glorious heart. The souls
that dwell in cities are cramped by the walls that surround them; but the eye of the sailor sees, beyond the
round bulge of the globe, the ports of foreign nations.
His soul expands with the expanse of sea and sky, and the
world is his home—he lives on it, and not in it.

Mark the young aspirant for literary fame. Fresh in
the world he knows but little of, he sees fame's temple
in the hazy sky, dreamy and beautiful,—and he must
enter. Glowing words and fiery fancies, or romantic melancholy and piratical gloom, he pours out for the edification of those of his own experience. Though he succeed,
his success is despised by maturer years. But oftener he
will fail, and fail by rule. We cannot write a book until
we have lived a book. Good books are not often specially
written for the market. They are incidental; and their
merit is often unintentional. There are books of the day,
and men who know how to write them, and who know
just how much they are worth. Verily the men have their
reward. They sit with their publisher, and smoke in his
easy chair, and commend him when he assures a new
comer with a manuscript under his arm "that it is not
always the best book that sells best." They will consult
the publisher as to what subject they shall treat next year;
talk of the "coming man," the "model" work; conjecture
what style of writing shall be next in luck; smile at the

success of ingenious puffing, and dub the generous public a vile pack of asses. Verily, they have their reward, and
they will understand our meaning.

You have seen an indigent mother of a large fam-
ily, with maybe a child at the breast, working the week
through. See her of a washing-day,—up to her elbows in
suds, her children quarrelling or complaining, her hus-
band away in dissipation;—with little to eat, and little to
expect, but every thing to do, what can be her compensation! "Bone-weary, many-childed, trouble-tried," what
can be her reward?—Think you she is wretched? Nay,
the soul rises to its mission, and fits her to her sphere.
With strength of body, or strength of mind, (for the
down-sick are seldom melancholy,) her body sweats, and
the soul grows calm and still. She hopes too for a better
world.—None but a laborer knows a laborer's compensation. We have stretched our limbs on the grass, of a
summer evening, and looking up at the mellow harvest
moon, have "wondered how earth could be unhappy,"
while labor is its own reward.

We remarked that the down-sick are seldom melancholy. When we are young, or full of life, death is
the king of terrors: he lends the eye a terrible aspect,
and we shun his presence. But when the life goes slowly
out, the less we have the less we care to live. The fading
consumptive walks slowly to his grave; he smiles at the
old jest; he listens to the old story, calm, and pure, and
still. The moment comes, friends gather around,—wife,
mother, brother, take him by the hand,—"he would not

leave them, but he is not afraid to die; he is going to a better world."

Even those little discontents of a personal character, wherein we weary of our own, and desire the peculiarities of others, find compensation and use. A man seeks a wife who has the merits which he lacks, and the man and wife are one in their posterity. Short men marry tall. Straight locks love the curly. Strong passions love the gentle; and the timid admire the confident and the brave. All this is excellent, preserving the harmony of the race. Should men love their kind,—big mouths marry big mouths, big noses marry big noses, stubborn men marry stubborn women, and so on, we might breed a monstrous perfection of parts, but hardly a perfect harmony of system.

And now, for the satisfaction of such as may fail to find the compensation of their entire experience, let us advance a proposition:—All successes may be classed as either carnal or spiritual, either in this life or in all succeeding lives. If he that thinks himself entirely unsuccessful in this life will believe, (what is not improbable,) that every succeeding life exists on a more spiritual plane, he will not fail to see that the training he has received—the carnal successes he has failed of, shall be compensated by the fitness he has acquired for that advanced position,—of which advanced position the faulty parts of his compensation are but the foundation for most reasonable prophecy. Then say:

We shall not complete life's compensation here, but

it shall wait for us at the threshold of the seventh—yea, the seventieth heaven. When this carnal race shall touch a more spiritual basis,—when its successes, its powers, and its places shall be won by the mind, rather than the body,—by the harmony of the soul, rather than by subserviency to corruption,—then many that are first shall be last, and the last shall be first. Then the fine madman, who was wise on earth only to wretchedness and neglect, shall surpass the soldiering brave whose thick head swaggered luckily through the world. Then the laborers of the heat of the day shall get more than a penny. Then many an humble saint, who daffed the world aside and lived a sacrifice to a determined purpose, shall rejoice at the early cultivation of those spiritual desires which alone can make knowledge available. Then the martyr who died true to his faith, though the faith may have been misguided, shall rejoice for ages in the courage that faced death so early and so well. Then many an unread bard and out-o'-the way student, unfit to wrestle with the brawling world, shall find their compensation, when the tasseled lord who dropped a penny in blind Homer's hat shall remind him of the charity, and crave the shadow of his fadeless laurel to shield his dim eyes from the light of heaven.

Then death, which a Frenchman pronounced "of all evils undoubtedly the greatest," shall appear of all blessings undoubtedly the most blessed, whose fear was all uncalled for,—uncalled for theoretically, as an event feared for its consequences. But we think men will ever fear death practically—"the sword that turns every way, to guard the tree of life." We shall "dread to die, yet care not to be dead." And "who would live always, away from his God?"

Section XVIII.

Pride, Labor, Experience, And Latent Pleasure

*W*hat better are all these truths which we have mentioned than subjects of consoling thought? Is not the infinite a hopeless study?—Then that is the greatest of all consolations which drives it out of thought altogether, and sets it at a convenient distance. Even though we think correctly, we may think too much. If this theology be the truth of God, there will be many minds incompetent to it: and it will be well if they have something to do, whereby they shall worry neither themselves nor the theologian with their incompetence. The infinite is a truth; the calculations of the almanac are truth; and this theology may be truth; and the conclusions of the latter may be useful, although many minds should be presently as incompetent to its processes as they are to the reason of infinity, or to the bases of astronomical calculation. It will be well if any thing shall generally preserve them from fretting over what they do not comprehend.

And as we examine man's position, in correlation with his limited faculties, we must be sensible of a divine charity which makes him for the most part careless of that which he cannot understand. Wavering between a thoughtless animal nature which exults in the pleasant sunshine and an intellectuality which at will (and at will only) glances off into the bottomless infinite which only the boundless God may encompass, how fortunate it is that, if he knows little, he cares little also! We know nothing of the first principles,—we know not the foundation of a single fact; yet this seldom troubles us. The globe floats away in its atmosphere,—we feel no alarm. Generations come, and look about them, and depart mysteriously into the ground, we all shall follow them,—yet do we plan, and dig, and dream, for the most part, with very little concern. We reproach one another's recklessness and extravagance, and follow his steps.—So divest man of this fleshly stupor that he should bethink himself continually of all that he really knows, and he would run into the wilderness, naked and mad.—We doubt not that there have been minds so bared from the bedozing influence of the flesh that they have at times stood almost against the actual,—men on whom the fact of existence and the miracle of nature glared night and day: and in this consciousness, knowing themselves different from, if not superior to other men, there have been bards, prophets, and madmen, who believed themselves especially inspired for a superhuman destiny. From all such genius may we be delivered. Luckier is the rude swain who "sits beneath the hawthorne shade, and carves out dials quaintly, point by point." The soul can wander to such ecstatic heights only to discover the incomprehensibility of God, and to tremble lest the seat of reason fall; while the more sensuous organization, more deeply wrapt in earthly desires and instincts, finds in the very depth of its existence a consoling assurance of its necessity, which amounts almost to a reason why it should live, and live forever. His vaulting curiosity and his fears alike are smothered in the gentle simmering of the flesh. His soul will not rush unbidden on the infinite; and the mystery of his unaccountable existence is forgiven and forgotten in the warm joy of existence itself.

To us, this carnal carelessness, or stupidity if you please, is a redeeming feature in man's life, here or hereafter. Wherever we exist, through a thousand progressive changes, we see this mantle of divine charity protecting us from the chilling winds that would otherwise blow in on us from off the vasty deep, where God walks, now as ever, alone. We believe in a "spiritual body," growing within this body of flesh, as a child grows in its mother, to be delivered into a finer sphere. And this new body shall lie down in the world to which it enters, and from it shall go forth another—and from this another—far into the depths of the eternal divinity. The soul shudders at any other existence than that of body—shudders at any direct partnership in God's majesty, and fondly clings to those carnal and spiritual bodies which hold us asunder, alike from the universe and him.

Founded upon and deriving its usefulness from the necessity of finite abstraction from the infinite, and from that useless self-contemplation into which, without some diversion, the finite will ever fall, is Labor. For this we are given desires and necessities, to provide for which keeps us occupied and diverted. Those who have not immediate necessities have ambitions, whims, and theories, to attain which keeps busy the ever-wakeful spirit. Without this diversion even all the beauty of the universe would pall upon our taste, and grow monotonous; and the latter draws us the more, because the former drives us. Thus the occupation of the hands and special faculties is made the rest of the general soul. And the soul must be driven into this rest, for it will not go of itself. Few men are so profound as to cultivate voluntarily all those works which the harmony of body and soul require. Many a luxurious liver, worn out with doing nothing, has wished himself compelled to labor in some capacity or other. Wealth would be a very excellent thing if it were free of that compensation whereby he that rejoices in his wealth is soon induced to neglect those things which are requisite to its enjoyment. But no sooner is the man turned to the enjoyment of his wealth, than some vile stimulus rids him of his health and spirits. Nine-tenths of your men of leisure spend their time in wavering between half an ounce of health and some means to get rid of it. And when they begin to feel the assaults of time, and labor under general debility, the last mean of recuperation is that which nature has specified—labor. They will take medicine enough; they will hunt for the best waters and the best air, and consult on the proprieties of diet,—try any thing but labor, which, after the first day or two, pays amply as it goes. Ah! my dear fellow, (says sarcastic Conscience,) any soup is good, if you will stir it well; and all waters are healing, were you as difficult in the coolness of the external as you are of the internal application.

But the great reason why man should labor is found in his natural consciousness of free-agency, whereby he gathers not only knowledge, but pride at his success. In spite of the intellectual acknowledgment of the omnipotence of God, man has a sense of independence which gives encouragement and dignity. This is as God will have it; our joy, ambition, pride, success, excite no envy in his bosom.

The utility of pride is very evident. Our fears of the future are based upon the unknown: and that which our own pains discover,—that which our own daring, or ingenious patience overtakes, is an assurance, in the consciousness of knowledge, under the divine delusion of free-agency, of the diminution of the external powers over us, and of our fertility of expedient in troubles unforeseen. The knowledge is not much in itself; but pride magnifies its attainment, and belittles the terror of that which we know not. A great joy is success. We rejoice, not so much in possession, as in possession by means of our own wit, patience, or labor. A fortune is but a fortune to him who inherits it,—a something to be valued at what it will do, buy, or bring: but to him who wins a fortune there is this compensation, that it is the representative of wit and energy which command fortune. What wonder then, when the thriving, toiling father loves to increase his wealth, while his prodigal son, who never earned an honest dollar, cares only to squander it?—The glory of all things to man is, not only that he may possess them, but that his image may be stamped upon them, and this superscription writ about it, "Mine by right of experience and labor."

It is the comfort and encouragement of this pride which guide and dictate the amusements of the people. Who go to prize-fights? Those who have something of the fighting ambition. Who read poetry? Those who are, in some sort, poets themselves. Who go to concerts? Those who go home humming the airs they have heard. We feel an encouragement in the successful performance of others, from a faith in our common humanity,—pride at the success of any man, since we are men ourselves.

And just here you will observe that the pleasure taken in the performances we have mentioned is one the capacity for whose enjoyment was acquired by experience, labor, or suffering in the past;—and it is consoling to think, when we are annoyed, suffering, or driven against our wills, that just so surely are we fitting ourselves for enjoyment hereafter,—acquiring latent happiness for future time to draw out. Who that can read, and has been charmed with the beauties of literature, ever remembered with pain the birch that assisted his urchin ambition? How well do we remember the heaven-attested oaths which predicated the broken bones of our venerable pedagogue when we should have attained ability for the task,—that pedagogue whose bones shall not be broken while ours can ward off the blow! Oh that we might not cease to remember that this is God training us to thank him.

A man takes no pride in any thing beyond his own experience. Increase his experience, and you increase his capacity for amusement, and his satisfaction with the world. There is a wide difference between a truth merely acknowledged in the mind, and a truth for which we have toiled or suffered.—Suppose you are conversant with the science of electricity,—it has been at some time your study, or your business, but now is not; casually you pick up a printed journal, and see an article headed "Effects of Lightning;" that article is for you,—you can teach its author, you will look to see if he understood his subject; and you spend a pleasant half hour over it. Beside this article is another, entitled "Draining Land." This is nothing to you; you are no farmer, and have no interest in the matter. Had you as much experience in draining land as you have in the laws of electricity, you had found in this paper another half hour's pleasure and pride, either in smiling at the ignorance, or exulting in the concurrence of its author. Life is full of these compensations of experience. Give us the night-key of a hundred theories, the toil-won skill of a hundred artists, the acumen of a hundred critics, and the world holds not a corner where we cannot be gratified. But who is this that travels without learning, or stands in leisure without having the memory of business? A wretched fellow doubtless:

he thinks to enjoy rest, and is not tired at all! A man of vast learning is never at a loss for diversion, and has never any time to throw away;—while an idle brain is "a workshop for the devil," being ever full of impatience and impertinence.

Dear Reader, we are not over-confident of having conveyed to your mind our own conception of the genius of the universe,—a conception difficult and tedious of utterance. We would have you see an infinite plenum, pervaded by an electric love: beating with an even pulse, infinitely charging and discharging—swelling here, and yielding there—sacrificing here, and favoring there,—changing for variety and new beauty, and returning to compensate, through ways as infinite and for reasons as infinite as the space it works in,—all things individually made and moved with reference to all other things collectively,—each thing having the epitome of all things in its own being, and all the universe covered with the influence of the simplest thing in existence, for whose pleasure all the universe is taxed.—Can you see our meaning? If not, let it pass as not all-important. But, what is more to the purpose, be slow to question the fairness of your own position in an existence which you do not profess to resolve,—be slow to suggest an improvement, ere you know what it is you would improve.

Section XIX.

Cross Questions
—Liberty And Heaven

$\mathscr{T}$hus have we found that God is doing at least all for us that we, after fair contemplation of the necessities of the case, can suggest in our own behalf. We have found that all intellects and powers must be fragmentary and sub-servient to God's single will. We have found that, to save us from wretchedness, the soul must expand. We have found that truth is the only means of that expansion. And we have found that through variety, mitigation, and compensation, the greatest possible knowledge, happi-ness, and progression are attained. We have found reason to believe that God is good. The old common-sense of men, which ever has favored this proposition, that evil is good, or else the devil reigns supreme, abides the test of ratiocination, which develops a simple theory, beginning with one God.

No man can deceive us in argument, nor lie with much plausibility, in short sentences; hence the severest test of truth is colloquial interrogation.—Before we go further, let us take time to quiz ourselves a little on the foregoing.

"Between these notions: that all is for the best,—that all past iniquity has been for the good of the race, and that, also, all future iniquity will be equally serviceable; and this, that all good is compensated with evil, as well as all evil with good,—there is no best course to take.—The universe is full of laws: were it not better that all men should observe them?—and if better for them, would they not be happier?"

Firstly then: we have spent our time in showing that all was for the best; that love reigns in the violation of law, even as in its observance, and that all things must work together for good, to them that love God, and to them that hate him, if such there may be.

Secondly: that all good has its price, as well as all evil, we are well assured.—Here! thou cowardly knave—up to the perilous breach, fight like a man, and soothe thy craven heart with the memory of one valiant deed!—He thinks the price too high. Here! thou ignoramus, bend thy brow over these dusty tomes, and after seven years' study, you will go where I go, and have pleasure in what pleases me! "Seven years! it will not pay me—the price is too high!"—Here! thou curmudgeon, comfort thy dying hour with the memory of one pecuniary sacrifice! But he thinks the price too high.—You think the price is low. You think a dollar in charity is well spent:—by so much as you give more easily than he does, by so much is your charity less a sacrifice than that which you ask of him. Give, give, until it shall require of you the effort which it requires of him to give, and then you will know the price of charity to him. You who are learned have passed your labor, and in your learning are more than compensated. But the ignoramus has a task before him. You say, a man is a fool to be less brave than you are: why more a fool than you, who are less brave than some other? He holds that relation to you which you hold to another: to be greater you must risk, tremble, and haply suffer. Courage without proof, like faith without works, is dead. Therefore good has its price: the bad and the weak think it high, but the good and the strong think it low.

Thirdly: "God has made laws: were it not better for all men to observe them,—and if better, happier?" As to happiness, if any man has found out a method for continual felicity,—if any man can show us how we may be even as happy continually as we can get in half an hour over a bottle of good wine, we will go ten thousand miles on foot to lay all our possessions at his feet, and on our knees implore of him his secret.—There is no such man, nor has such a method been discovered. We have seen no man of whom we could affirm a happier fate than our own. You will find some men sacrificing the animal to the spiritual; and some are sacrificing the spiritual to the animal. We cultivate the golden mean; yet it is a low-toned sort of world—no one is continually exulting.

But when you say "One course is better for me than another?" we answer, yes: yet when you ask us, what is that course? we answer, that is to be determined only by your taking it: you cannot go amiss, while God reigns. The course that you will take will be the best course for you, and for all other men.—"Is it not better for me to obey the laws? and if better, happier?" If you obey, it is better than to have disobeyed; if you disobey, it is better than to have obeyed,—and if better, happier.— "But what shall determine me?"—God.—"But I would be happy."—And you shall be as happy as possible.— "But what shall I seek?"—What you desire.—"By what means?" By all the means you know.—"Shall I seek for knowledge?"—You can not avoid that knowledge which is best for you.—"But there is such a thing as a wise man, and such a thing as a fool!"—Aye—but there is no such thing as a wise man making a fool of himself. According to his wisdom he will obey the laws. "But if he disobey, will it not be the worse for him?"—No. He is not wise as yet, if he disobey: but if he disobey, it is better, for this will make him wise. It does not follow, because a wise man will observe the laws, that a fool would find that course the best. The policy of the wise is wisdom; the policy of the fool is folly, until he become wise,— for "wisdom is foolishness to the simple." "But the best course is the happiest?"—Aye; and the fool takes the best course, for a fool. Every man has the wisdom of God for his own salvation. "But the way of the transgressor is hard."—And the stolen fruit is sweetened with liberty.— "And is the wise in his wisdom no happier than the fool in his folly?"—Were it not unjust that one man should be happier than another? Is it not better, if there needs to be a variety, that one quality should compensate another in the general consciousness of men? And for the fact, question experience. Is not the fool the jolliest of us all?—By common consent, the fools do the laughing, and the wise look on. Ask yourself, are you not wiser than when you were a boy? You are. Are you not freer? You are. Are you proportionately happier? You are not. Yet you would not go back, save you might take your wisdom with you. Therefore all you have gained has not made you happier, but it has kept up the tenor of your consciousness. For this is the nature of progression, THAT THE SOUL GROWS WITH ITS FORTUNE.—"If I am no happier now than in boyhood, it is because I neglect what I have learned, and violate the laws of my being."—This brings us around again to a former position in our treatise: that the advancing growth of the soul must prefer knowledge and variety, pleasure and pain, to any monotonous course whatsoever. Why do you not retain the innocence of childhood? Why does not Adam keep his Eden? Because it is ignorant, dull, and tame. Why is it dull and tame? Because of the expansion of the soul.—"If I chose to obey the laws, I might be happier than when a boy."—Then why do you not do it?—"Because I am a fool, I suppose!"—Precisely so: and if you are less happy in this your present course of life, is it not the pain of it that will soonest drive you out of it, with ample store of worldly knowledge, into a course more steady and wise?—"It would seem so."—Then is not folly the policy of the fool?—So wisdom is the policy of the wise. *Why should a man suffer twice, to learn one fact?*—Would you defeat this notion, that all is for the best, put your hand in the fire and burn it well: then you will say, "This is all for the best, with a vengeance!"—Truly it is. You will say, you have made a fool of yourself: on the contrary, you were a fool beforehand, and should by this be wiser. It was a lesson that a wise man should not have needed. So of all these aches and pains which come of man's love of excitement, novelty, and general diversion: when he learns so to live in voluntary self-command that he shall not have forced upon him unneeded wisdom, (which we doubt will ever fully transpire,) then that self-restraint will be the sole requirement, price, or compensation, of continual tranquillity. Then man's soul will not be under the law; he will be a law unto himself, and he will live by faith. That for which the law was given, variety, sin, diversion, having become unnecessary, man is no longer in bondage. Then nothing is impure in itself, but to him that esteemeth it impure, to him it is impure. There is no law over the magnificent Paul; let him eat, let him drink, let him riot; he may suffer, but he cannot sin, he cannot offend conscience. Then all things will be lawful, but all things will not be expedient. Then, in the calmness of the true and only religion, he need not laugh like a boy, he need not smile,—nay, he need not be even happy, as the sensual world knows happiness; but mindful of all laws of his being, glorious in sacrifice, glorious in pride and magnanimity, striving more and more after that universal benevolence in which lies the brightness of all his glory, he shall scorn the joys and fears of baser souls, and pain shall not shake his fortitude again. Then shall he cry, in triumph, "I raise my head bravely toward the threatening rock, the raging flood, or the fiery tempest, and say, I am eternal, and I defy your might! Break all upon me!—and thou Earth, and thou Heaven, mingle in the wild tumult, and all ye elements, foam and fret yourselves, and crush in your conflict the last atom of the body which I call mine! my WILL, secure in its own firm purpose, shall soar unwavering and bold over the wreck of the universe: for I have entered on my vocation, and it is more enduring than ye are; it is Eternal, and I am Eternal like it."

The heaven of progression is the home of liberty. Not liberty to follow with impunity the dictates of an obdurate heart,—but liberty by will and reason from the control of all unprofitable desire, which now annuls the wisdom of the world. And to this liberty we are growing forever; to this all things inevitably lead us.

Liberty is the idol of the soul—the burden of every prayer; it is the gold of gold, the beauty of the beautiful, the strength of the strong. The soul is in fetters, and struggles to be free.—O! bannered War, and death-defying Courage! why are ye the glory of the earth? Why do fame, wit and fortune bow down before the hero? The poet sings him, and the artist paints him, glorious to themselves as heralds of his glory. The pride of art, and time, and weary labor, fades at the sudden coming of that vehement discontent which, in ancient fable, first hung the holy heavens in sorrow, when the brow of Lucifer uprose to scorn and anger. It is not for the love of slaughter in itself, nor hate of man's creations,—it is not for envy of ill-gotten wealth, nor hate of beauty, when we see the soiled maid trampled in the bloody earth, besmirched and spotted,—the works of genius littered from their classic shelves, and temples tumbled down, where the owl may hoot from ruins at the cold and solemn moon,—no! but it is for the spleen of weakness, and the hate of foreign power,—the time-old wish for freedom,—the wish to triumph over law and form, to teach all majesty in the wild school of liberty, and to glorify in spite the worm that fattens on the greatness that oppressed us. Not in the outer world—in the unsatisfactory treaty in the heedless aggression, of themselves considered, shall we seek the motives of this turbulence; it comes from the reproach of the genius within.—Behold the tumultuous fray! hear the voices of the captains and the shouting, the neighing steed whose neck is clothed with thunder, the bickering steel, the banners flapping in the wind! From the turrets of yonder city the eyes that shall be weeping look down in exultation at the courage of such flesh as they are. Is it for right that struggles beneath the heel of oppression—is it for the gaze of streets-full of heads which shall greet his triumphal entry,— is it for tears that shall dampen his valor's grave, made holy land forever, that yon pale madman in the smoke of war's exploding thunders chides on the warhorse with his barbed heels to bound over the dying, though it be to die? No—it is a poet this—a self-consumer; he seeks the ancient joy—to have looked death in the face, and felt he never shall be daunted more. Labor is nothing, nor poverty, nor pain, nor loss of friends or kindred to his eye who ever triumphed over a field of battle, or held the dying hero with his face against the foe. The world is his, and it was made for him—the valley green, the waving plain, and the far, dim steeps whose weird abnormity shall catch peace from his presence.

There is a liberty of Alexander, when he has conquered the world; but the liberty we seek is the liberty of Diogenes, when he has conquered himself. The first is liberty in defiance of law; the last is liberty above the law; he asks no other favor of the conqueror of nations than that his glory should not obscure the light that shines upon his path. This is the liberty of progression. Perfect liberty we may not have, nor perfect serenity: we shall stagger—but we are staggering towards the throne. We shall not reach it: never shall we know the meaning nor the end of this eternal life; but what though we may not comprehend the universe—what boots the circumference, when each of us is the centre, and the apple of God's eye? What boots the goal? what boots the prize? *To win* is all: the race its own prize, for there shines on it "the star of the unconquered will." Then rise, O! soul,—up and onward forevermore!—The difficulties never will diminish: struggle now, O! gladiator of the world, and through toil and bereavement, through tribulation and anguish, you shall rise like a planet in the glory of the Lord.

Ever be mindful that God is with you. Never dream that he and you have a divided interest,—for, as much as you can conceive him, he is father, brother, friend. Think not you can oppose him, or that he can ever cease to love you. Nay, more: strike out into the world; do or die—*which*, it makes far less difference with you than you ever have believed. Put faith in God—put faith in your destiny—assume the positive—live with force and freedom; and the more you go at the bidding of the lofty genius that prompts the royal hours of every man, the nobler and the holier will be your life. What is bread, or wine, or debauchery, or fame—what is all that passion craves, or fancy covets, beside the daring presence of that ever-blessed peace, the soul of honor,—

That "more true joy Marcellus exiled feels,
Than Cæsar, with a senate at his heels"?

Section XX.

Immortality Inferred

$\mathcal{S}$een in the light of this theory, is there any thing in nature that does not fit some purpose, and do some good? Look at the plain necessities of the soul, and then at the variety and compensation which fill those necessities as far as the harmony of the universe and the good of all will permit, and then let us ask ourselves, is the soul immortal?—If it be not, we shall not be extant to complain; but is there not a plain intention that we shall be extant, and rejoice thereat? We have filled none of our ideals; we have accomplished nothing; not two men in a generation attain a mental balance. We come in a hurry—we whirl through our lives—we scarcely ask whether the earth is eternal—and away we go, full of an infinite speculation—certain of some things, doubtful of most, and all this to no further purpose than to keep up this fruitless race!—There is no objection to our living again—we desire to live again—yea, we all think we shall live again. It is useless to say that the notion of immortality was first suggested by some impostor: God was the father of that impostor, and there was purpose in his existence.—What!—after all—all our speculation, all our hopes and ideals,—after all the promises our theory affords us, that whatever can be done for our pleasure will be done, is it probable, reasonable, sane, any thing but monstrous, that God, like a boy who draws an image on a slate, wantonly spits on us, and wipes us out? We cannot believe it. Give us a segment, and we can describe the circle. Give us a bone of an animal, and we can describe the animal. And if this segment of life would fit a glorious imaginary circle, either that circle exists, or else the only thing that lives in defiance of all analogy— the only thing whose instincts are opposed entirely to its interests, is the human soul. We cannot think that God would put it into the head of a frivolous squirrel to provide store of nuts and leaves for his first winter, and leave us, whose poring brain has ached over his providence, to run through folly into shelterless and everlasting shame. Nay! we too shall be cared for—we shall succeed: in the softening gales and sunshine of a coming Spring, this first rude tenement of the soul shall be blown away, and she will leap and laugh in a rejuvenated world.

Section XXI.

The Policy Of Life Is Harmony With Nature

$\mathscr{S}$till it is an open question, and as such falls under the judgment of practical reason. Here then is the sure policy of man: We must assume that FITNESS TO THIS WORLD CONTAINS THE EMBRYON FITNESS TO ALL WORLDS TO COME. If there be other lives, it is improbable that they exist in any contradiction of the policy of this. The harmony of nature forbids the supposition that he who moulds his being in conformity with the laws of this life is preparing himself for degradation in the next. And so clear and forcible is the propriety of this conclusion, when fairly considered, that we may say with confidence, the knowledge of the harmony between nature and man is the knowledge of the true religion of this world.—Another truth follows, equally cogent: we see that men differ in opinion,—which difference argues a difference of construction, or of bias: Then the method of attaining the harmony between nature and one man must differ from the proper method between nature and another man,—and of this difference every man is properly his own private judge.

Now inasmuch as man consists mainly if not entirely of two principles, the animal and the spiritual—the mortal and the immortal,—(or, if spirit be denied as an independent essence, then of two tendencies, one to sensuality, and the other to spirituality,) then we must believe that the difference in men consists somewhat in the relative proportions of these two principles or tendencies. There must be a golden mean, or average line of being, dwelling in the just proportion of these two principles or tendencies, from which line varieties branch off, only for the purpose of variety as heretofore explained. There is one style of human being nearer in harmony with nature—nearer in the due proportion of animal and spiritual forces than all others. What is that style of being is an interesting study; there may be room for experiment, also, on the proper method of attaining that style.

A general idea of what any age esteems the true symmetry of human nature will be gained from an examination of their religious notions, and the aims pursued in their education of the young. In the beginning of the Christian era, courage, strength of body, fortitude, and truth, were the noblest of attainments,—and this strength and greatness found their proof only in the field of battle. But Christ taught men that it was nobler to suffer blows than to give them,—as, indeed, it requires more fortitude and general magnanimity,—and this magnanimity was to be proven by consistency with conscience in a spirit of universal benevolence, in defiance of suffering, danger, and death. The great heart of humanity swells with holy emotion at the memory of this Glorious Being, the only recorded embodiment of man's ideal of moral greatness. Men have disputed whether he was God or man; he was *of* God doubtless, (if that may mean any thing,) born for an immortal destiny, and a name that shall stand ever first in the calendar of human names. That he was the One God, however, we cannot believe: yet there has been no other such man. His doctrine lives, in proof of his lofty nature.—Nor are we about to offer any objection to that doctrine as now understood; but we shall question the foundation upon which that doctrine is properly grafted—the proper condition of the mind before it should act upon Christ's precepts.

It is not astonishing, as history chronicles the horrors of barbarism and ignorance, to find mankind seeking hope and comfort only in the opposite direction. Man swings from one extreme to another and now it is reckoned the height of civilization, when there is but a breath of opposition to the notion that all men indiscriminately should be cultivated in the direction of suavity and intellectuality. It is taken for granted that all men are too selfish, too thick-skinned, thick-skulled, arrogant, cruel, and obstinate,—and that proper cultivation consists, without exception, in softening the hard, refining the coarse, and rendering pliant and amenable the stiff and stubborn. And that treatment which would fit the ancient Romans, with all their courage, combativeness, destructiveness, and bodily strength, is assumed to be equally applicable to entire modern nations who may, perhaps, lack a sufficient foundation of these Roman qualities to give a firm basis for the superstructure which Christ taught men to build.

Men are forced to acknowledge in practice, however they may fail to recognize in theory, the mighty social power, for good as well as for evil, of that predominance of animal spirits—that warmth and vehemence of personal feeling which in excess comprises what is called *passion*; and although this passes in theory as at least a questionable quality, the entire want of it is subject to contempt among those whose teachings dread to give it countenance. Nature will out. We know in our hearts, however we may mutter with our lips, that there is a manhood above all intellectual ingenuity,—greatest in generosity, but great even in depravity,—greatest in Jesus of Nazareth, but great also in Alexander of Macedon, which appeals to us as the actual of a cherished ideal, and comforts the frailty of our common nature like "the shadow of a great rock in a weary land,"—a manhood that dwells in self-possession and defiance of pain. There is a glory of the sun, and a glory of the moon; there is a glory of the moral, and a glory of the intellectual nature; and, proud or humble, the same God is father of them all. Aurelian, splendid beneath the pillared arches of shouting Rome,—Latimer, at the stake,—and the poor gladiator, his nude chest heaving on the sand, and his full heart bursting with love and death as his dim eyes roam towards the banks of the Danube, to the great heart of humanity are one. Citizen or countryman, it matters little,—where bred—where taught—where travelled matters little,—the place subserves the man. Wherever the hero stands, he stands a column, and he stands alone. The orbed world is but the pedestal of his beauty. No rags can unman him—no pitch can defile him,—for every defect of outward circumstance looks but the random jeer of that fickle Fortune who cannot beat the brave, for all the gods despise her.

To say that the education of this age aims at the attainment of any measure of this moral greatness is to speak of it more favorably than it deserves; on the contrary, the indiscriminate culture of the modern mind is one which tends to an opposite result, and must drive most men still further into their present general extremity. Our experience has taught us that while many minds are too deep in the flesh, there are many more that are not deep enough; that while many are too selfish, mulish, and obtuse, there are others too sensitive, sentimental, and delicate; that while many are too proud, bold, self-willed, and aggressive, there are others too lowly, timid, conservative, and retiring, judged either by themselves or by any standard which reason will accept, or the ideals of humanity countenance.

We have spoken before of the utility of that passion stuff—that obscuring, stupefying flesh, the conjunction with which alone could make finite intelligence tolerable. As we look upon man in the abstract we must be sensible of a proper balance in the relative forces of the spiritual and the carnal, in making up the consciousness of the individual. We all know men enough both over-spiritual and over-animal: and there are whole ages over-animal, and ages over-intellectual—of which this age is one. (Not that there is too much intellect in the absolute,—but too much in proportion to the moral and animal force of the race.) And when we undertake to cultivate ourselves or others in the formation of character, we must judge of the material we would work on, before we begin to mould it differently. And we will do well if we find no fault with any man, though he be seeking an opposite extreme from what we are, whereby what are his virtues may appear vices to us, and would be vices if by us adopted. One man may seek to increase, and another to diminish the passion-stuff in their respective compositions, with equal virtue and piety; but such is the narrow dogmatism of this age, and mainly of all ages, that, upholding some special set of rules, men dictate their own necessities as the virtues of all other men, unmindful of the variety and self-dependence of the race, and in defiance of an old and excellent proverb, that one man's meat is another man's poison. "Let not him that eateth not judge him that eateth."

There is a limit of intellectuality in the native capacity of every man, above which exercise may suddenly carry him too far; and the instances of this excess are as notorious as those of its opposite. What is this we hear of *the melancholy of genius*, but confirmation of our truth? Should the perception of beauty make a man sad? or is it the brain overwrought, the digestion spoiled, and the

whole nervous system prostrated, which do the mischief? Bacon and Copernicus, Shakspeare and Milton,
these were not melancholy men, for they were men of
temperance, and healthy brain. But Rosseau, and Byron,
and Keats, and others of the hot and solid brain, and the
unhealthy blood and nerves, have been melancholy from
over-exertion, or personal excess.

Equally notorious are the instances of derangement
in the direction of conscientiousness. Void of the proper
confidence and tranquillity of life, men have been driven
out of their wits by fear from some trivial dereliction. Men
have been too good, as well as too bad. The Christian
world has applauded the sturdy moralist who approved
"a good hater." He was a man of the world, in the highest sense of that expression. He had struggled to compe-
tence and distinction through poverty and neglect; and
he had gained, for he needed, strength. He knew that,
in this world, to be tranquil we must be tough: he knew
that modesty, gentleness, and benevolence are better
when assumed from principle than when coerced by native impulse; he knew that it is good to breast the tide in
the love of contest and of effort, and to be generous and
amenable while the great soul stands ready at a moment's
warning to say *no*, to the death. He knew that man must
stand, if he stand, or fall, if he fall, alone. Alone he comes
into the world, bald, sniveling, and toothless, to live and
grow and decay in body, before God; and alone in his
second childhood, as bald, as sniveling, and as toothless
perhaps as in his first, he lies down to die, and his experi-

ence and his philosophy alone can give him hope, while, speechless and impotent, he judges all the earth.

We love to see our children shine: it is intellect that glorifies the world: but we forget in our eagerness to develop it that only nerve and energy can make intellect effective and serene in this jostling and contentious life. There have been more successes in the world by reason of nerve and perseverance than by reason of extraordinary subtilty of understanding. The ages are full of great intellects, unknown of the race for their want of confidence and persistency.—There is no sadder sight, to us, than intellectual precocity. The fine-grained, delicate organization, with an eye of fire, a hot brain, and cold, damp feet—the fond hope of short-sighted parents, urged on by them to shun all recreation, and to struggle for the prizes of the class, blooms early, but fades in the heat of the summer: he never fulfils the promise of his boyhood. It is said of him, "Ah! if he had lived—he died early."—But the knotty headed, hardy visaged urchin, slower to learn, and swifter to do mischief,—a boy in his boyhood, waiting for his manhood before he plays the man, may grow to a ripe old age, calm, honorable, and wise. Nor need he be a blockhead either. Many of the great of the earth have passed for numskulls in school, because they grew so slowly. Yet in all that we know of growth, slow growth is the best. It is not the long leaping and the lofty vaulting which make the athlete. These are but the expenditure of that force which long-continued moderate exercise, with patient care and cleanliness, has developed. Far better is it that the childish soul be kept warm and dreamy in its pleasant flesh, and slowly brought to light with a view to making a good and happy man, than to be rashly expanded like a thin bubble, to glow for a moment with some rainbow promise, and then to burst into the upturned and admiring eyes of its projectors. How often this eager haste has written on the mournful monuments of genius, "whom the gods love die young!"

And had we the wit and patience to restrain us, we are all of us living too fast. This is part of the youth of our immortality; we have no need to hurry, for there is time enough, and we shall miss nothing by waiting a little. Many of us touch bottom in this life at five and twenty, and thenceforth grind our weary feet upon the gravel. Sometimes men mourn for their lost youth: but why did they not enjoy it while they had it,—while the senses were warm, and the light of the eye turned all things into gold? They hurried to manhood, they hurried to gray hairs, and now, they would they were a boy again. They would carry the wisdom of age back into the innocence of childhood, and make childhood happier than ever it was, forgetting that the wisdom of another age will condemn the haste and impatience which find no contentment in this. Time wears thinner and thinner that emotional substance which separates us from the Almighty. In our infancy we sleep away the greater part of our time; and as we grow older, we sleep less and less. We are working out from the dozy material into the thoughtful spiritual; and we doubt not that at some time during every stage of our advancement we shall look back upon our more material life with the eyes of a more thoughtful existence, and wish that we had calmly and wisely lived in obedience to its laws—because we had wit enough, we think, if we had cared to use it. We shall sigh after these days, now lost in discontent and bootless aspiration: we shall call them the happy, happy days—days of dream, and sunshine, and peace: we shall remember how the nights bent over us, cool and beautiful, when the garish day was gone out and forgotten,— how the crystal dew came down, distilled in silence from the spray of stars,—how the young winds came from the untravelled waves and shook our love-locks asunder;— ah! we shall tell how it was not wisdom nor the love of wisdom that made us happy, but we were in harmony with nature—fresh from her hand,—we smelled of the warm brown mould from which we sprung,—but from which harmony the thirst after an infinite experience lured us too hastily away.—Boys we would be men; men we would be angels; yet the sure policy of every grade lies in patient conformity to its laws.

It will be good for some to cultivate these earthly desires which call the mind away from reverie and speculation, to the comprehension of the divine benevolence and the glory of nature. How beautiful is all the world! for what reason, if not that we may love it? How it draws us, lest our thoughts fly too far from it!—Our strongest affection is for those whom we must leave upon it; our strongest passion is that which leaves our image after us, when we sink into its bosom. Question its peculiarities, and its wonders: why has the ox a split hoof, and the horse a solid one? What is that necessity which numbered the digits up to nine, and made all nature pay that nine respect? What is the reason of all that calls us to examine? There is but one conclusion: it is to arrest and to divert us, to coax and to banter us sulky sons of God.

There are religionists to whom those ornamental arts which dignify the present life for its own sake are impertinent and unworthy. Yet when the soul has reached any degree of self-possession, beauty becomes a desideratum of its peace. All God's labor is for beauty and for love of beauty; there is little of man's hope in the world but to see and to create beauty. A conception of the brevity of life is made to frustrate the utility of the beautiful; yet who believes in the brevity of life? "Men think they cannot live now; they are to live hereafter; "they never are, but always to be blest:" but what is a coward but a coward, even in heaven? If any life is noble, this life is noble. We may observe all laws, yet court all that is lovely in the universe. This is religion: to resist temptation, and not to avoid it; it is not to hate life's poetry and hug the prose,—to take by choice the crust of the "bread of life,"—to close our eyes against a thousand charms, to stop our ears against a thousand harmonies, to bury ourselves in brown homilies and black bombazine, and forever to ruminate in silence and solemnity, while the blue steel of heaven bends over us in vain; this may be to hate the devil, but it is not to love the Lord.

Especially do the true proportions of the carnal and the spiritual find an expression in that aggregate wisdom of the middle classes, known as *common sense:* a wisdom which takes calm and healthy views of things—which respects well worn opinions, believes in proverbs, brings its precedents, and has faith in past experience and success; a conservative wisdom, sceptical of untried and brilliant isms, less from contempt for what is new than from content with what is approved,—less from dislike of change than from dislike of that lean and hungry vanity which is the motor of most innovation. It has the merit of steadiness and consistency, and is, more than any thing else, the balance-wheel of society. It doubts incorporated benevolence, especially when vented abroad; and its home charity is spiced with a certain brusquerie which furthers this truth, that the best way to lighten a burden is to stiffen the back that bears it.—An excellent thing in society is common sense. It minds its own business, and has no faith in "boiled mutton and near relations." It is not disputatious—fast to agree or to disagree, but has an honest self-respect which is the charm of all intercourse. Nothing can be more insipid and unnerving than conversation with a person of no antagonism,—one who agrees by halves to sentiments which he does not entertain, and all but swallows his opponent in eagerness to assure him when he coincides.

And in society, even as amid the beauties of nature, man should be capable of fearless scrutiny and enjoy-

145

ment, and especially be capable of doing his good purpose through all tribulation and strife. Man is the greatest of curiosities; and man is most curious in his excited and abnormal conditions. But from these conditions fly away the timid, perhaps with the hypocritical consolation that they are too civilized to be brave. Wavering between what they know men to be, and what the books insist they themselves ought to be, every hour of what they design to be honorable lives brings their ideal in collision with their personal fears. The proud override the weak, and they would rebuke them, but dare not. Ruffianism is abroad, and every day bears witness to injured innocence. Accident and neglect put human life in daily jeopardy; yet their assistance and personal risk never attain their own standard of true heroism and self-sacrifice. They groan under their own condemnation.— And shall we say that by *they* we mean nearly ten tenths of all those who profess above other men to be followers of the brave, self-sacrificing Jesus? Trace the recorded instances of noble daring and devotion—see who have sprung forward in the hour of peril, and risked their lives to save the perishing;—not many pious, not many godly of this world are called—but James the carpenter, and Peter the fisherman—fellows without the pale of superfine intelligence and so-called moral refinement—these are the men who tread the tottering plank, who rush through smoke and flame and bring forth the dying into life,—these are the men whose daring rises with the storm,—who climb the breaking mast,—who hold the tiller while their arms are burning,—who live in monuments for deeds whose beauty none saw so clearly as those who failed to do them.

Benevolence is good,—refinement is good,—gentleness and suavity are good,—and above these, socially considered, modesty is good; but without assurance, resolution, and self-respect,—without that foundation of manhood which can make these virtues *yours, instead of you,* they will be void of any great utility to society, and comparatively a curse to their possessor.

We shall not make so little of the discretion of men as to point out those courses and methods of education which will correct this over-intellectual and immoral age. Men know the proper methods—they lack but the true philosophy to tolerate them. But we will add a fable:

Of old a little man prayed Jove to make him mighty. And Jove heard his prayer, and said unto him: Mortal, behold I commit into thy hand this single bolt of thunder; hide it about thee,—and strike but thy most formidable foe.—Thus armed, the little man rejoiced, and feared not, and the world gave back before him. A hero he lived; and in a gray old age, lifting in his hands the unspent bolt to heaven, he cried, Behold, O! Jove, thy minister unused! The confidence of divinity is as divinity itself.

—◈—

The Future

No truth shall fall: but, weary of their load,
    Fear's haggard pillars shall lie down; and the owl,
Hooting the pilgrim on his ruined road,
    Shall mock his twilight stories of the soul.
I see far vistas, to be man's abode,
      Where bell funereal never more shall toll,
        Nor cypress quiver;
I see the flashing of the splendid wave
That makes the posies grow on Error's grave,
    Along Life's river.

The Son of Man, at length the son of woman,
    Brother of all men, and the Prince of Peace,
Grafts on the solemn valor of the Roman
    His Christian sweetness, and the wit of Greece.
Men see at last the race hath many a Saviour,—
    They see the royal majesty of love,—
They see, too, the magnificent behavior
    That blends the daring eagle with the dove.
      No law shall fail,
Nor sanction truculence and lust of blood,
But give the sturdy villain for his good
    The stripes that heal.—

Over the fallen thrones
Of intellectual empires passed away, —
Over the mossy bones
Of Superstition's weird and sombre sway,
I see the sun of human glory rise.
I see the Spartan mothers
Lead forth their stately sons,—
I see a thousand Howards,
And a hundred Washingtons.
From many a creed-bound shore
The human surges roar
"Men shall be bondmen never, never more,"
And freedom's clarion wakes the golden skies.

———

THE END

4511119

Made in the USA
Charleston, SC
02 February 2010